GRADES
2-4

Teaching Students
to Conduct Short **Research**
Projects

Ryan K. Gilpin

**Mini-Lessons to Help Students Write Successful Research Reports
from Start to Finish and Meet Higher Standards**

■SCHOLASTIC

New York • Toronto • London • Auckland • Sydney
Mexico City • New Delhi • Hong Kong • Buenos Aires

Dedication

To WMG, How sweet it is . . .

Acknowledgments

In life, it's important to have good mentors: those who teach you; those who inspire you; those who encourage you; those who challenge you; and finally those who believe in you. Through the years I have been blessed with amazing mentors and without their influence I wouldn't be the teacher I am today.

First there is my Aunt Martha, whose stories about teaching inspired me to follow in her footsteps at a very young age.

To my teachers, Mrs. Harrell and Mrs. Edmundson, who were there for me as I began to figure out who I was and where I was going in life. Thank you for encouraging me to follow my dreams.

Mary Wyman opened her classroom to me as a student teacher, allowing me to begin my journey as an educator. Thank you for teaching me the ins and outs of classroom management.

Brenda Boyd and Diane Koon taught me more than I ever learned in college as I stepped into my Head Start classroom as a first-year teacher. Thank you for constantly challenging me to improve my craft.

And finally to Laura Robb, thank you for all of your support from day one at Powhatan. Thank you for teaching me, inspiring me, encouraging me, challenging me, and for believing I could do this at those times when I myself did not!

To my husband Billy, thank you for the countless hours you spent listening to my ideas and reading my drafts. Without your help and support this book wouldn't have been possible, and I still wouldn't know the proper use for a semicolon!

To my good friend and colleague Cheri Kesler, thank you for letting me bounce ideas off of you and talk through this book as I was writing. Hopefully the other gym goers weren't too bothered by our chats while on the treadmill!

To my parents, you all are truly the best. Thank you for always supporting me. Dad you always said it and I never really believed you, but you were right—I am a writer after all!

Lastly, I would like to thank all of my students through the years for being my guinea pigs as I tried new ideas and for being willing to take the necessary risks with me as we learned how to research together!

●　●　●　●　●

Cover Designer: Jorge J. Namerow
Editor: Joanna Davis-Swing
Interior Designer: Sarah Morrow
Copyright © 2015 by Ryan K. Gilpin
All rights reserved. Published by Scholastic Inc.
Printed in the U.S.A.
ISBN: 978-0-545-65336-7

1　2　3　4　5　6　7　8　9　10　　40　　23　22　21　20　19　18　17　16　15

Contents

Introduction

I love teaching. I can't imagine having a career doing anything else. Some might even say it's in my blood—I am, after all, a fifth-generation teacher. In my family, teaching dates all the way back to the early 1800s in a small one-room schoolhouse in Stowe, Vermont. For me, teaching is fun and exciting; I love that no two days are ever the same! It is sometimes stressful; I work long hours, and I am always thinking about teaching even when I am not in the classroom. But every morning when I enter my room, I look forward to the day I'm going to have with my students. I have always loved learning new things, and I get to share my love of learning with others every day. For me there is nothing better than watching a child have an "aha" moment when he or she has learned something new. Knowledge is a gift, and I am privileged to give my students a gift that can never be taken away.

How This Project Came to Be

When I was first hired to teach third grade, I had many ideas for projects I could do with my students. After reviewing the curriculum, I saw that students were to complete a project on a type of owl. I was really excited about this project because I love owls and have been fascinated by them since I was a young child. As I went through the materials that had been left for me, I realized what the students were to complete was more of a written report. Looking through past reports, I noticed that they all followed the same format. I realized that students had very little choice about how to craft their report. I was impressed with the writing, and the amount of information students had gathered was incredible, but it seemed as though there was very little room for creativity, something I strive to foster in my students. As a new teacher, I was afraid to make too many changes to how things were done, so my first year, I completed this owl report with my students just as it had been left for me to do. But it felt wrong in some way. There was no driving force behind the research; my students didn't know why they were doing the project, and the reports showed no individuality. Sure, they had learned more about crafting nonfiction features, paragraph writing, and text structure—and a lot about owls—but they weren't overly motivated, and by the end they were ready for it to be done!

That summer I decided my goal for the following year was to branch out from this project but still meet the standards and expectations of learning. I read numerous books about reading and writing nonfiction and about project-based learning. After completing my own research, I knew that I could meet the requirements set by the school while making the project more engaging for students and allowing their individuality to show through their projects. My overall goal was to incorporate student choice throughout the project while addressing the standards I was required to teach.

The first major change I made was to allow my students to choose any animal they were interested in as the subject of their research. I also added key questions to help focus students' investigations. I then decided this would not be a traditional, formal report but instead it would be a nonfiction publication. This would open the door for my students to have a choice in what they were researching and give them the opportunity to explore the various ways nonfiction can be presented. After learning about different types of nonfiction texts, they would have an opportunity to choose which one they would like to create, which features of nonfiction they would like to use, and how they would set it up. This again would provide students choice while they were learning about nonfiction writing.

When I first conducted this project it went very well—the students were motivated, understood why they were researching an animal, and shared their learning creatively. In fact, no two projects looked the same, and I met the teaching requirements! After reflecting on the process, I realized there was so much more I could do, especially with technology, and I decided to add even more options. Now I allow students to create slideshows and PowerPoint presentations and use a document publisher so the final projects can look like actual magazine articles, plus I've added many more ideas that my students have come up with. I feel as though this project will forever be evolving and continuing to get better.

Meeting Higher Standards

Today's higher standards place greater emphasis on nonfiction reading and writing. These skills are important because they not only build incredible content knowledge but also because they increase vocabulary development. Short research projects develop students' abilities to read and write nonfiction while also effectively engaging and motivating students to learn the essential skills and strategies the rigorous standards expect.

How to Use This Book

In my classroom I follow the workshop approach for reading and writing, so the lessons in this book were completed during that instructional time. In the chapters that follow, I will walk you through teaching students how to conduct short research projects—everything from introducing what research is, to choosing a topic, selecting sources, taking notes, and planning, writing, and revising a final product. The final chapter addresses publishing and presenting the finished work. The lessons follow the gradual release model: I demonstrate during a mini-lesson, offer students the opportunity for guided and independent practice during work time, and I bring students together at the close of the lesson to share their learning.

The lessons in this book are designed for students in grades 2–4. As I walk you through the lessons, I'll be providing examples and sample conferences from my third-grade class. But remember, these lessons can be adapted and differentiated as needed.

Mini-Lessons

Each session starts with a whole-group mini-lesson. In the mini-lesson, I introduce the skills or strategies I want my students to focus on that day or over the course of a few days. I model the tasks I ask students to perform, always allowing opportunities for questions and sharing ideas.

When I am modeling, I ask students to get comfortable and to be active listeners. That means their eyes and ears are on me. I am also very careful about how I speak while modeling, being selective with my words and actions. Before modeling, I think clearly about what my purpose is, what skills I will be focusing on, and how I want to convey the information to my students. During the modeling, I frequently pause and ask students what they notice me doing. This helps them to reflect so that when they are using the skill independently, they can remember more clearly what I did. Most of my mini-lessons follow the same format: I introduce the skill, allow time for discussion, model how to use the skill, and then recap before explaining the activity or task that students will do during work time.

Work Time/Conferencing

Most lessons in this book include a section called Work Time/Conferencing. In this section of the lesson, I share typical conferences I have had with students to guide them through the research or writing process, to practice skills introduced in the mini-lessons, and/or to address common needs that come up year after year when students are conducting research. When conferencing, I try not to give students the answers but rather to guide their thinking so that they discover the answers on their own. My main form of assessment comes through conferencing with students. I have a conferencing notebook in which I take notes after each conference. This helps me keep track of who is where in the research process, what specific needs they have, and goals I have set for them. At the end of each day, I review these notes to help plan upcoming lessons, small-group lessons, and future conferences.

Sharing

Most of my lessons include a sharing component. Sharing is usually one of my students' favorite times of the reading and writing workshops as it allows them the opportunity to share their learning from that day immediately with their peers. It also reinforces the skills or strategies from the mini-lesson. In the sharing section, I provide either conversations we have had as a class or an activity I had the students complete in small groups. Often I preselect who will share with the whole group so that points I want to reiterate or new strategies specific students discovered can be discussed with everyone.

Conducting Research Projects

Over the years I realized that when my students do research, they aren't just learning content; even more important, they are learning how to find answers to their questions and then share their newfound knowledge with others in a meaningful way. Although I may have a product in mind, I always allow for a lot of choice. For example, when I had my students create a museum about the *Titanic*, they were able to choose what they wanted to learn more about and what to include in their display. When I do a biography project, students choose who they want to study, plan their own displays and costumes, and prepare for a live interview as their subject. It's never just about the actual product, but instead also about the process students undertake to create it.

I have conducted a number of research projects with students, and each time the product was vastly different; however, the process was the same. I have five simple steps that my students follow in order to complete a project, no matter what the product is:

- Narrow the focus and develop a key question.

- Conduct the research.

- Create a plan for the product.

- Put the plan into action; create the product.

- Present and share the learning.

Each chapter in this book contains lessons that correlate with and support these steps. In Chapter 1, *Getting Started With a Research Project,* my lessons focus on step one of this process. Through four lessons, you will see how I get my students thinking about research, how we choose subtopics for research, and how to develop key questions. This step allows students to establish the driving force behind their research. In Chapter 2, *Conducting Research,* I offer four lessons that show how students gather information and evaluate and document sources. In Chapter 3, *Creating a Plan,* I share how I get students planning the product they will create, which is a nonfiction piece. In Chapter 4, *Putting the Plan Into Action*, I present five lessons that focus on the writing process and nonfiction writing. Chapter 5, *Publishing and Sharing,* covers the last part of the process, when students create the final product and present and share their learning with others. In this chapter, I provide four lessons that focus on publishing and public speaking skills.

To illustrate the research process, I use a perennial favorite as an extended example—the animal research project. However, each lesson can be adapted for any research project you choose. In the Appendix, I list other projects I have done with students following the same five-step process, along with different publication and presentation options.

MAKING IT YOUR OWN

I hope that you will find this book helpful when doing research projects with your students. When I read books like this, I hardly ever use the lessons step-by-step or word-for-word. I do, however, look at the lessons and think about how I can adapt them to fit my style or the needs of my students. When reading through these lessons, think about your own teaching and your own students and consider how these lessons could work best for you. I hope that as you are reading, you will feel inspired to try something new or think about your own teaching in a new way.

One of my favorite things about working with children is that they are so curious about the world around them. They look at their surroundings with fresh eyes, and their ability to ask a million questions about everything around them never ceases to amaze me. Conducting research projects with students is a great way to foster that curiosity while at the same time providing incredible opportunities for children to grow as thinkers, readers, and writers.

Getting Started With a Research Project

Conducting research is a complex undertaking that requires very specific skills. It's also an exciting process, and I always play that up when introducing students' first research project of the year. To help them learn about the research process, I establish parameters: I provide a general content-related topic, a theme, and some key questions. For the lessons in this book, I share examples from an animal research project. Students are free to choose any animal to research, and they explore the theme of survival to help focus their research. Of course, the process is the same no matter what topic you choose; you could easily incorporate research projects into units on the solar system, weather, natural disasters, current events, U.S. presidents, states—the possibilities are endless. In the Appendix, I share other research projects I have conducted successfully with my students.

Before students begin any research-based project, they must understand exactly what research is, what tools they can use to conduct research, and how to focus their research. This chapter will serve as a guide to help you get your students started.

First, it is important to find out what your students already know about research. Have they done research projects in the past? Have they had some experiences where they had to conduct research? What do they remember and know about doing research? Lesson 1 focuses on the collection of this information from your students.

After reviewing what research is, it's time to have students choose a topic and begin thinking about what they already know about their subject and what questions they have about it. Then students can focus their research by developing a key question. The next step is to teach students to organize the information they collect by creating categories and subcategories related to the larger topic and key questions. By taking the time to do these things with your students, you'll ease them into the project with a clear idea of how they'll be researching their individual topics and what specific information they should be looking for.

Chapter 1 Lessons

- What Is Research? (2–4 Days)
- Choosing a Topic (1 Day)
- Developing Key Questions (1 Day)
- Creating Subtopics to Support Key Questions (2 Days)

Lesson 1: What Is Research? (2-4 Days)

Before students begin their first research project with me, I assess their prior knowledge. My goal for the mini-lesson is to find out what my students already know about doing research and what they think it looks like. By gaining a better understanding of what, if any, research experiences they've had, I can better prepare future lessons and gather appropriate materials to use throughout the project. After the mini-lesson, I schedule one or two extra conferences to help students with less experience get started.

The two topics covered in this lesson can be broken into two days if that suits your students better. For example, on day one you could cover the question *What is research?*, and on day two you could discuss different tools for research. With some classes I have been able to put the two together, while with other classes I've provided them separately. Students spend the additional days reading widely about the general topic.

MATERIALS

- Chart paper and marker
- Books at various reading levels related to research topic
- Conferencing notebook (see page 13)

Mini-Lesson

Mrs. Gilpin: I told you this morning that today was a big day! It is time for us to begin our animal research project. But before we begin I want you to think about a question. Remember that thinking means taking time to create a picture in your mind, brainstorm ideas, or make a list of different thoughts. I don't want you to raise your hand quite yet because I want you to really think this through. So here are my questions: What is research? What do you do while researching? What does doing research look like?

I give students time (usually about a minute or so) to think quietly before we begin the discussion. There is always at least one child who wants to share right away and I just redirect him or her to think more about the question. This allows those students who need time to think through their answers a chance to do so.

Mrs. Gilpin:	Okay, now we are going to share our thoughts. I'd like for you to turn to the person next to you and share what you were thinking.

I give students two to four minutes to share.

Mrs. Gilpin:	Would anyone like to get us started with what we think research might be? Maria, what do you think research might be?
Maria:	You pick something and research it.
Mrs. Gilpin:	Yes! You pick a topic. I'm going to write that here on our chart paper.

> ### Teaching Tip
>
> *Having students turn and talk gives everyone the opportunity to share their thinking. Some students will share with a partner, but not in a whole group.*

As students share their responses with the whole group, I write them down on a large piece of chart paper hanging on an easel.

Dan:	It means you learn about the topic.
Mrs. Gilpin:	Great. We'll add "learn about the topic."

As I write on the chart paper, I read it aloud to the class to repeat the information shared.

Doug:	You find out information.

By this point the students have given me some key words that go along with doing research, so I take a moment to emphasize them.

Mrs. Gilpin:	Great! We will add "find information" to our chart. We're getting some good words here: *topic, find, information,* and *learn.*
Aubrey:	When you go on the Internet and you type in your topic and find stuff about the topic.

Some of the children are beginning to share how *we might research. I make it clear that their answers are important, but that they should save those thoughts for later when we discuss tools for research.*

Mrs. Gilpin:	Great thinking, Aubrey! When we research we may go and look something up on the Internet. There are lots of tools we may use for research, and we're going to get into that in a few minutes, so keep that idea in mind, and I'll come back to you.
Phil:	Read about the topic.
Mrs. Gilpin:	Yes, you might read about the topic.
Simon:	Well, we had that author here, and he wrote nonfiction about sports. He had to know a lot about sports.
Mrs. Gilpin:	You're right, and when Henry Cole was here, he said that when he is writing a book he does what?
Students:	Research!

Now my students have made a real connection to research by remembering what author Henry Cole shared with them. As I go through what the author shared with us, I point to the key words on our chart so that students can see the connection between what he did and what they will be doing as researchers.

Mrs. Gilpin: Yes, Mr. Cole does research for his books, which means he's learning more about his topic. He's finding information and reading about the topic. So what happens when we are doing research?

Liza: You learn more stuff about something you didn't know!

Dan: You find interesting facts!

Once the chart paper has many of the key words I want students to connect to the idea of research, I give them an actual definition of what research is.

Mrs. Gilpin: You know, I think you all have some really good ideas here about research. You're on the right track and have used some key words: *topic, learn, find, information, interest.* All of those are key words because when you are researching something, you begin by picking a topic. Then you go and find, or gather, information about that topic. As you find information, you begin to learn about your topic, and the more information you find, the more you learn! Now, some of the information you find will be new and some of it you might already know. But even if you already knew that information, researching might deepen your understanding.

> **Teaching Tip**
>
> *If you haven't had an author visit, you can always visit author websites or search for author interviews to give students a sense of how writers work.*

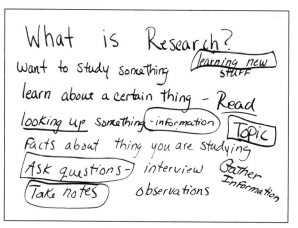

Anchor chart on "What is Research?"

At this point, depending on the class and how attentive they are, I may stop the mini-lesson and allow students time to read books about various topics they will be researching. Otherwise, I continue the lesson.

Mrs. Gilpin: Now I want you to think about what tools we can use for research. Aubrey, you shared with us earlier and I told you to hold on to your thought. Can you share with us again?

Aubrey: I was saying that you can go on the computer and look things up on the Internet.

Mrs. Gilpin: That's right! The Internet can be a tool for research because it is a place where we might find information about our topic.

Eliza: Books! We can read books about our topic.

As students share, I write their responses on a new piece of chart paper titled "What tools do we use for research?"

Mark:	Newspapers.
Ben:	And encyclopedias. They have a lot of information.
Lea:	What about asking people, like my mom. She knows a lot about science.
Mrs. Gilpin:	Lea, what a great idea. When researching, you might interview someone who knows a lot about your topic. That is also a tool for research.
Liza:	Well, I watch *Animal Planet* sometimes and they have information about animals a lot.
Mrs. Gilpin:	Yes, Liza, they do, so let's add "TV" and "movie clips" to our list of research tools. There are some great video clips I am going to share with you later on about animals.
Mary:	*Ranger Rick.* I was reading about kangaroos.
Mrs. Gilpin:	Great thinking, Mary. Magazines could be a place where you find information, so I will add that to our chart.

I usually stop after we have six or eight tools on our list and review them with the students.

Chart with tools for research

Mrs. Gilpin:	These are all great tools that we will be using when we start our research. In fact, we will use some of them today.

WORK TIME/CONFERENCING

Next, I introduce what students will do during their work time. When starting a research project I like to spend a few days focusing on the larger topic students will be studying. This allows them to get to know the material better and ultimately to find something within that topic they are interested in learning more about.

Mrs. Gilpin:	During your work time today and tomorrow, I would like for you learn as much as you can about various animals. That means I want you to read about more than one animal. That way, when you finally decide which animal you want to do your project on, you'll be certain it's something you are really interested in.

I have a lot of books and magazines laid out on the tables. I want you to take some time and browse through them, and then I want you to pick one or two to look through. You may already have an idea of what animal you'd like to research, but take some time to look at information about other animals too! Let's take about 15 to 20 minutes to read, and then I will begin conferencing with you.

Children peruse the various books and magazines. As they make their selections, I stand next to the tables to help any struggling readers make appropriate choices. I make sure to provide materials at a wide variety of reading levels, so each student has the opportunity to choose a topic he or she will be happy with and to research it using texts at an appropriate level.

After students have begun looking through books, I circulate through the room to conference with them about their reading, asking questions to further their thinking about the animals they are reading about.

Mrs. Gilpin: Hi, Doug. I see that you're reading about hamsters. What made you decide to pick up a book about them?

Doug: Yeah, well I love my hamster, Rex. I'm just not sure I want to do my project on them. I don't like this book that much, and I already know a lot since I have one.

Mrs. Gilpin: There are so many animals to choose from. Are there any you don't know a whole a lot about and would be interested in?

Doug: Well, cheetahs are cool, and tigers.

Mrs. Gilpin: Did you get a book about either of those to look at? Maybe you could look through books about cheetahs and tigers to see if you find one of those more interesting than hamsters. Let's go to the table and look to see if we have any books about tigers or cheetahs.

In my conferencing notebook I make a note to check back with Doug the next day to see if he found either of those two topics more interesting. As I continue to conference with students, I make notes about what they are reading and what I may want to follow up with them on.

Mrs. Gilpin: Hi, Eliza. I see you're reading about elephants.

Eliza: Yeah, and they are pretty cool.

Mrs. Gilpin: What are you finding so fascinating about them?

> ## Teaching Tip
>
> *Recording conference notes in a conferencing notebook is an invaluable tool. For each conference, I note the student's name and record brief notes about what we discussed, what the student is trying next, and what areas need to be addressed in the future. I review my notes at the end of every day to look for patterns and ensure that I'm meeting each student at least twice a week. I also make note of students I want to be sure to check on at the beginning of the next class.*

Eliza:	Well, they are so big, and the babies are so cute. Look!
Mrs. Gilpin:	They are really cute! Have you read about any other animals yet? It's always good to read about more than one topic; that way, when you make your choice you know you will be happy with it and excited to learn more about it.
Eliza:	Yeah, I read about beavers too. It was kind of interesting. They build dams, and I saw one on the river one time. I really like the elephants, though. Can I keep reading about them?
Mrs. Gilpin:	Yes, absolutely. I hope that when you decide on your topic you're really excited about it; so keep reading!

SHARING TIME

During sharing time students have the opportunity to talk about some of the facts they learned from their reading. This allows them to hear interesting information about a lot of different topics and helps encourage them to read about new topics the next day. As students begin to share, I encourage them to ask one another questions. As I wrap up our workshop, I bring back some of the key words from our mini-lesson.

Ideas for Building a Classroom Library

Over the years I've expanded my classroom library tremendously, with a special focus on informational texts to help with research projects. Below is a list of ways you can build a library without spending too much of your own money.

* Visit yard sales, rummage sales, flea markets, and used book stores.

* Check out eBay and other online auctions, along with sites such as freecycle.org and half.com.

* Ask your local community library if they have an annual book sale and/or what they do with books they are removing from their collection.

* Order from book clubs, such as Scholastic—you can earn bonus points for each dollar you spend. You can then use your bonus points to buy more books!

* Ask parents to donate any books their children do not want any longer.

* Contact your Parents Association; they may give money to teachers for special projects.

* Contact community organizations that may give grants to teachers for special projects.

* Talk to the school librarian. At the end of the year he or she will most likely discard books from the collection.

Teaching Students to Conduct Short Research Projects © 2015 by Ryan K. Gilpin, Scholastic Teaching Resources

Mrs. Gilpin:	Today you read about many different animals. Would anyone like to share an interesting fact they found?
Lisa:	Bats are nocturnal.
Maria:	What does that mean?
Lisa:	They are awake at night and sleep during the day.
Phil:	All sharks aren't dangerous.
Simon:	That's cool! I didn't know that! I might do sharks!
Mrs. Gilpin:	Wow! It sounds like you all found some very interesting information while reading today. You learned a lot of new facts about animals, and it sounds like you each might be well on your way to choosing your topic!

It's important for students to have a wide range of topics to choose from, so for two or three days (sometimes more), I let them continue looking through books and other materials. They share the information they've learned with friends and peers, and they write about it in their writing journals.

Lesson 2: Choosing a Topic (1 Day)

After discussing research and research tools and giving students time to explore various materials about our subject, I ask them to choose a specific topic to focus on. Some students will have known from the start what they want to research, while others have many topics they would really like to explore. Through conferencing, I help students decide on one they will definitely be excited about. Lesson 2's mini-lesson is very short and simply explains to students what they will be doing that day. The conferences with each student are key to this step of the project, because often students really need help narrowing down their choices.

MATERIALS

- Books at various reading levels related to the research subject
- Paper and pencils
- Conferencing notebook

Mini-Lesson

Mrs. Gilpin:	The last few days we have learned about what research is and talked about the tools we use for research. You have also explored a lot about different animals. Today, you get to choose which animal you will research for your project! The first thing I want you to do is make a list of the top three animals you might like to research. Then I want you to take some time and think about which of those three you really would be excited to research. After that you can decide which animal to

choose. Once you have made your decision, you will do a little writing for me. In your writing journal, write a paragraph about the animal you chose and why you want to research it. You may also share some interesting facts you have found so far. If you are unsure which animal to choose, you can continue reading about your top three choices. I will be coming around to conference with you about your choice or to help you pick from your list.

WORK TIME/CONFERENCING

I give students some time to write the list of their top three choices before I begin conferencing.

Mrs. Gilpin:	Hi, Dan! I see that you have a few animals on your list that you are interested in choosing. Which one do you think you like best?
Dan:	I'm not really sure. I really like honey bees and they are interesting, but chameleons seem interesting too.
Mrs. Gilpin:	What are you finding so interesting about chameleons?
Dan:	I want to know why they need a tail and why they change color.
Mrs. Gilpin:	Do you know more about one of those animals than the other?
Dan:	I already know a lot about honey bees because we have hives at my house. I don't know much about chameleons. Maybe I should do chameleons since I don't know much. Plus, they look awesome.
Mrs. Gilpin:	It sounds like you are really interested in chameleons. I want you to keep reading about them and I'll check back with you in a bit to see what you have decided.

I give students who I may need to check back in with 5–10 minutes to work before returning to them. During that time, I conference with others.

Mrs. Gilpin:	So Dan, have you made a decision about which animal you're going to pick for your project?
Dan:	I've decided to do chameleons since I don't know much about them. The books are more interesting, too.
Mrs. Gilpin:	That's a great decision. I think you are going to be fascinated by some of the facts you learn.

After students pick the topic they want to research, I have them write a paragraph in their writing journals informing me of their choice and why they decided on that topic. They also share what they hope to learn about the topic. I allow time in class for this, but have also assigned it for homework.

SHARING TIME

My students love hearing which topics their classmates will be researching and asking each other questions. For this lesson, I allow enough sharing time so that students can each share their topic and one question they hope to answer while completing their research.

 Teaching Students to Conduct Short Research Projects © 2015 by Ryan K. Gilpin, Scholastic Teaching Resources

Mrs. Gilpin:	Today is an exciting day! You finally decided which animal you will be researching. We are each going to share with the class our animal and a question we hope gets answered. Carter, we'll start with you.
Carter:	I picked sharks. I want to know how many types there are in the whole world.
Maria:	I picked dolphins, and my question is, where do mother dolphins have their babies?
Tim:	I picked honey bees, and I want to find out how long they can live.

Once everyone has had a chance to share, I allow the students time to converse about their topics and ask one another questions in small groups.

Student writing about his selected topic in his writing journal

Lesson 3: Developing Key Questions (1 Day)

When students begin researching, it is important for them to narrow their focus so they can identify a clear purpose for their research. This makes the task of organizing their information easier. One way to help them narrow their focus is by deciding on an overall theme and key questions for the project. Key questions create the driving force behind the research. They help students to understand why they are researching a particular subject. Why should they care?

For the animal research project, I selected the theme of "survival" due to its connection with our science curriculum. The overall focus will be finding out what the animals need in order to survive and what role humans play in the survival of the animals. My students will help decide what information they need to explore related to this theme, and we'll develop a series of questions they will find answers to. I also give students the opportunity to develop their own questions to answer while gathering information.

During work time, students are given time to just read about their topics, which builds their background knowledge and gets them engaged in their learning.

MATERIALS

- Chart paper and marker
- Books, magazines, and websites at various levels related to research topic
- Conferencing notebook

Mini-Lesson

Mrs. Gilpin: Now that you have selected an animal to explore, we need to figure out what type of information you should be gathering. It is important that you have a key question or theme related to your topic to help you to focus your research. That way, you know exactly what type of information you should be searching for. For this project, we will focus on survival. We will focus on what your animal needs in order to survive in the wild, and what role humans play in the survival of animals. What do you think of when you hear the word *survival*? What do we need to survive? Take a moment to think about these questions and turn and talk to your neighbor about your ideas.

After a few minutes, I invite students to share with the class.

Luke: We need food. So do animals.

Niv: Water.

Ana: A house. We need a house, and animals need nests and stuff!

Carter: I need my mom. She takes care of me.

Mrs. Gilpin: It sounds like we need many things to survive, and so do animals. Now I want you to take a minute and think about what we learned when we studied animals in science. Think about what animals might need to survive. As you begin to share your thoughts I am going to write them on the chart paper.

Lea: Shelter.

Liam: Like fat. Something with their body.

Mrs. Gilpin: Yes! There is a word from science for that.

Niv: A physical adaptation.

Luke: I remember that turtles having a shell is an adaptation.

Mrs. Gilpin: Yes! We learned a lot about physical and behavioral adaptations in science, so I am going to write that on our chart.

Ana: We learned about animal groups, too. Like reptiles, mammals, and fish.

Mrs. Gilpin: Great, let's write that down on the chart.

Bill: Their defenses.

Simon: Good smelling or hearing.

Mrs. Gilpin: Wow, you all are on a roll! I'm going to write that down too, Simon! Anything else you can think of about animals and survival?

Phil: What they eat and food chains. We learned about food chains and webs in science.

Greg: Other animals.

Katy: Getting enough food.

Eliza:	Eggs. Birds lay eggs.
Niv:	Predators trying to kill prey.
Evan:	Behavioral adaptations.
Greg:	An animal running away.
Simon:	What about habitat? We should find out where our animals live.
Mrs. Gilpin:	One thing that I think we all know is that animals need a variety of things in order to survive. As you are reading today I want you to think about what your animal might need in order to survive. Now I want you to think about another question: What role do humans play in the survival of animals? What are humans doing to help animals, and what are humans doing that might be negatively affecting the survival of animals?
Katy:	People litter, and birds can eat it, and it can hurt them.
Evan:	But people also pick up trash on the roads, and that can help.
Pam:	Yeah, litter in the ocean can hurt fish. I read that in the dolphin book.
Liam:	Sometimes people hunt when they aren't supposed to.
Greg:	My Dad hunts on our land, and we use the meat.
Phil:	There are laws about hunting.
Eliza:	My mom puts bird feeders out when it snows. She says it's so they can still get food.
Mrs. Gilpin:	These are some great ideas! Humans can help animals, but they can also threaten them. We will be exploring this idea further as we research our individual animals.

As students share ideas, I write the ideas on the chart paper. Once our list has many of their responses, I end the mini-lesson and give them time to read about their topics. We will use the information we collect in the next lesson as we create categories that go along with our theme.

WORK TIME/CONFERENCING

Mrs. Gilpin:	I can see that you all learned a lot about what animals need in order to survive from your books and from what we learned about animals in science. This is really going to help us as we each begin to learn more about one animal. As researchers, it's important to figure out what type of information would make the most sense to share with others. Tomorrow we will use this list to create categories to help you with your research. Now I would like for you to continue reading about your animal and getting to know it better!

I usually give students 20–25 minutes to read about their individual topics. When that time is up, I ask them to think of some questions they hope to answer about their animal in relation to our theme. Once students have had some time to write their questions, we gather so they can share with each other what they are interested in learning more about.

SHARING TIME

Mrs. Gilpin: I know that I asked you to write questions you had about your animal yesterday, and today I had you take some time to think of a few more. This time I want you to think about your animal and the word *survival*. What questions do you have about how your animal survives in the wild? Who would like to share a question you have? You can also share questions you wrote yesterday.

Evelyn: When moose are attacked, maybe by wolves, what do the moose do?

Katy: Why do dolphins react like people? They are really smart animals. They can do some of the same things we can do, like catch balls. They can answer a trainers' questions. How do they do that?

Evan: Do octopuses eat nautiluses?

Mrs. Gilpin: These are great questions. I hope that as you are researching you find the answers to them! When reading, you can look for specific information to help you find the answers to these questions. Does anyone else have a question about your animal you hope gets answered?

Niv: What types of dinosaurs are peregrine falcons related to?

Greg: I want to know how snakes get their venom.

Mrs. Gilpin: I love your questions, and I know that you can find answers to them as you are researching. When researching, it is important to have a clear focus on what type of information you're looking for. Tomorrow we will look at the list we created about survival and create questions and categories to help guide our research.

Some of the questions students ask are simple and their answers are easily found, while others are more complex and students may struggle to find the answers. Our next lesson will focus on creating subcategories for research based on our list, and then we will develop questions for each. In Chapter 4, I will present a list of questions for students to explore to help support higher-level thinking and to use when writing a paragraphs. Providing support in developing these questions in the early grades allows students to become more independent in this task as they get older.

Lesson 4: Creating Subtopics to Support Key Questions (2 Days)

One of the biggest challenges for my students as they begin researching is organizing the information they find in meaningful ways. To help with this task, I teach students how to create subtopics as a way to break down their large topics into smaller parts. This strategy not only helps them to organize their information, but it also makes the project seem less overwhelming. As we create subcategories, I continue to reiterate the overall theme or key questions so students make the connections. I like to do this lesson before they learn how to take notes so that when they begin note-taking they understand how their notes should be organized.

Day 1: Creating Subtopics

MATERIALS

- Chart paper and markers
- Chart from previous lesson with the theme of our research
- Books, magazines, and websites at various reading levels related to research topic
- Conferencing notebook

Mini-Lesson

Mrs. Gilpin: Yesterday we talked about the key questions to help guide our research. Our theme is *survival*, and our key questions are: *What do our animals need to survive in the wild? What role do humans play in our animals' survival?* We also created a list of things we think animals need to survive. Today we are going to look at this list to create subtopics that will help us organize the information we find while researching. Take a moment to read over the list and start thinking about how some of these things could be related. You may discuss with your neighbor the connections you are making.

At this point I have the students go through the list they created to determine how this information could fit into categories. As they look at the list, they start to sort the ideas into categories such as food and diet, adaptations, life cycle, *and* habitat. *As they make these connections, I start a second chart of these new subtopics.*

Mrs. Gilpin: I can see that you are starting to make connections to common subtopics. I'd like for you to share some of the connections you have made, and as you do I am going to start a new list on this chart paper with these topics. Can someone give me one connection they made while looking at our list from yesterday?

Evelyn: Well, it said *homes* and *nests*.

Pam: Yeah, where our animals live.

Mrs. Gilpin:	Great! So we've seen that some of the things on our list are about where each animal lives. Think about what we learned in science, what is that called?
Evan:	It's called *habitat*.
Mrs. Gilpin:	Yes, I am going to add "habitat," or where your animal lives, to our new list. What were some other connections you made?
Elizabeth:	There is a lot about food.
Liam:	Yeah, there is food, water, predator, and prey.
Bill:	Food chains.
Mrs. Gilpin:	I am hearing that animals need food and water. I am also hearing you mention how they get their food. I'm going to add "food and diet" to the chart as another subtopic we will research. Let's keep going.
Niv:	We talked about adaptations, like physical ones.
Mrs. Gilpin:	Yes, as we learned in science, animals have many adaptations to help them survive, so I will add that as a subtopic to the chart.
Beth:	And cheetahs, they run fast. That's something they do.
Mrs. Gilpin:	Yes, we learned about behavioral adaptations too! Let's think of some more things we learned in science.
Aubrey:	What they look like.
Evelyn:	Yeah, like its body.
Mrs. Gilpin:	Okay, so I am going to add "appearance" to our chart.
Niv:	We also have babies and eggs.
Evan:	It says family.
Mrs. Gilpin:	I'm going to add "life cycle" to our chart. We will be looking at how our animals are born and at their family life.
Aubrey:	What about litter and pollution? What people do that hurt animals.
Mrs. Gilpin:	We did talk a little about that yesterday. There are many threats to animals caused by humans. I will write "threats" on our chart as well.

By the end of the discussion we typically have the following subtopics listed for research: habitat, food and diet, appearance, adaptations, life cycle, *and* threats. *After this discussion I explain to students how they are going to continue to research their animals. I have books, magazines, and websites ready for students to explore as they start to gather information.*

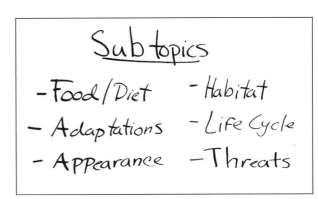

Our chart of subtopics

Teaching Students to Conduct Short Research Projects © 2015 by Ryan K. Gilpin, Scholastic Teaching Resources

Mrs. Gilpin:	Let's look at the list we created and the subtopics you will be researching about your animals and what they need to survive. We have *habitat, food and diet, appearance, adaptations, life cycle,* and *threats.* Today you will again have time to read about your animal, and as you are reading I would like you to think about these categories. After you have had some time to read we will gather again and discuss some facts you have found about your animal and look at our chart to determine which category the fact would fit into.

Teaching Tip

Use a bookmarking tool to keep track of websites you want students to visit. You can organize links by topic and hide them from students at any time. Do an Internet search for "social bookmarks for teachers" and explore options that might work for you.

WORK TIME/CONFERENCING

I again give students about 20–25 minutes to read without taking notes. While they read I try to meet with every student to ask about what he or she has learned so far.

SHARING TIME

For sharing time, I start by having students turn and talk to their neighbors, thus allowing everyone to get a chance to share. Then, I call on four or five students to share some interesting facts they have learned with the whole class. As students share, we look at the chart we created and discuss which subtopic each fact would fit with best.

Shelia:	I learned that marsupials have pouches for their babies. I think that might be life cycle since it's about babies.
Phil:	Sharks have big teeth.
Simon:	That could be appearance since it's what they look like.
Katy:	Dolphins, they live in the ocean. That's habitat.
Mrs. Gilpin:	Wow! It sounds like you all are learning a lot about your animals already! Tomorrow we are going to look at each subtopic and decide what information we need to find for each and soon you will be ready to start taking notes.

Day Two: Developing Questions Within Each Subtopic

Part of the challenge for students when researching is determining what type of information they should be looking for within the subtopics we select. Creating a list of questions and specific kinds of information they should be gathering helps them complete their projects to the fullest. It also helps them organize their information.

MATERIALS

- Chart with subtopics and marker
- Books, magazines, and websites at various reading levels related to research topic

- Sticky notes
- Conferencing notebook

Mini-Lesson

Mrs. Gilpin:	Yesterday we decided on some subtopics to research about our animals and what they need in order to survive. Today we will look at each of those categories and decide what type of information we should look for or questions we should try to answer. Let's start with *habitat*. What type of information would fit best there?
Niv:	Where our animals live.
Evelyn:	Its home.
Mrs. Gilpin:	Great! I'm going to add two things to the chart, "Where in the world can my animal be found?" and "What type of home does it have?" For example, does it have a nest, den, or burrow? What else could we add?
Evan:	How they make their home?
Mrs. Gilpin:	So I will add, "How does my animal make its home?"
Beth:	The place: like hot, cold, desert, and rain forest.
Mrs. Gilpin:	Yes, I'm going to add the question "What type of environment does it live in?" For example, does it live in the forest, rain forest, freshwater, saltwater? Let's look at the next category, *life cycle*. What types of connections did you see on our list, or what types of things should we look for when researching this subtopic?
Simon:	How it's born.
Doug:	Yeah, like some are born and some hatch.
Mrs. Gilpin:	Let's add "How is my animal born? Is it a live birth or does it hatch from an egg?"
Dan:	And if it stays with its mother.
Pam:	If there are more babies. Like the mom had like five puppies.
Mrs. Gilpin:	I hear a few things so I am going to add, "What is its relationship with its mother like?" "How long do they stay with their mother?" "How many babies are born at once?" Anything else we should add?
Katy:	Maybe its life, like when it dies.
Mrs. Gilpin:	I think that is an important thing to bring up. We should find out what our animal's life span is, or how long it lives. I will add that as well.

We continue this discussion until we have filled in questions or important points to research for all of the subtopics we decided on in the previous lesson. Once we have completed this, I start a discussion about humans and the role they play in the survival of animals.

Mrs. Gilpin:	Now that we have discussed the things animals need in order to

Teaching Students to Conduct Short Research Projects © 2015 by Ryan K. Gilpin, Scholastic Teaching Resources

survive in the wild, I want you to think about humans and the role we play in the survival of animals. Are there things we do to help animals survive? Are there things we do that hurt animals? One subcategory you will focus on is *threats*, or what types of things are going on that could hurt your animal.

Eliza:	I read that my animal is endangered.
Doug:	What does *endangered* mean?
Mrs. Gilpin:	If an animal is endangered, it means that not many of the animal are left, and the animal might be close to becoming extinct. This is something you should all explore about your animals. I'm going to add the question "Is my animal endangered?" to our subtopic of *threats*.
Simon:	What about hunting? Hunting can make an animal endangered, right?
Dan:	There are laws about hunting.
Mrs. Gilpin:	There are many laws that try to help protect animals. In your research you should try to answer the question "Are there laws to help protect my animal?"

I add the questions to our chart.

WORK TIME/CONFERENCING

Mrs. Gilpin: Now you are going to begin gathering information related to these subtopics. As you are reading I want you to think about these categories we listed on our chart today and how what you're reading might fit into one of them. If you find facts about your animal that you think fits into one of the subtopics on the chart paper, like *habitat* or *life cycle*, I want you to mark the page you're reading with a sticky note and write that subtopic down. That way, when you start taking notes you will be able to find your information more quickly. I will be conferencing with you to help you do this successfully throughout your work time.

Habitat- Where in the world Can my animal be found?
Environment- Climate Hot Cold
Desert, Forest, Water
-Home/shelter Tundra, Artic, Grassland
-How do they make their home?

Food/Diet- What does my
How much? animal eat?
How do they get their Food?
Food Chain Herbivore
Omnivore Carnivore
Predator Prey
Scavenger

Questions for our subtopics

Students then begin to read, researching their animals. If students are using a website, I have them use their writing journals instead of sticky notes. In their journals, they make note of which websites gave information on these subtopics. After about 10 to 15 minutes of work time I begin to conference with students about the information they have found so far and to help them mark pages with sticky notes. By marking pages with sticky notes, they will be able to take notes more efficiently since they will easily be able to find facts they want to include in their writing.

Mrs. Gilpin:	Hi, Eliza. I know yesterday you were very excited about picking elephants to research and I can see that you have quite a few books about them here. What kinds of things are you learning about them?
Eliza:	I just learned that an elephant is pregnant for 18–20 months. That's a long time.
Mrs. Gilpin:	Wow! That is a long time! What subtopic do you think this fact would fit best with?
Eliza:	I put *life cycle* on it since it is about moms and babies.
Mrs. Gilpin:	Great! Now when you start taking notes you will know that page has information about life cycle on it.

This next conference is with a child who is struggling to figure out what subtopics go with the information he is reading.

Mrs. Gilpin:	Doug, what have you learned so far about cheetahs?
Doug:	Well, they have spots and they run fast and they have cubs.
Mrs. Gilpin:	I can see you are learning a lot about cheetahs. Let's look at your sticky notes and see what subtopics you have to go with these facts.
Doug:	I don't really have them since I wasn't sure what to do.
Mrs. Gilpin:	Okay, let's see what we can do. Let's look at the page you're reading. Can you read this paragraph and tell me one thing you learned?
Doug:	It says that cheetahs live in Africa.
Mrs. Gilpin:	So it looks like you have found an interesting fact. Look at the chart we created with the list of categories we're researching. Do you see one that this fact would fit with?
Doug:	Yes, I think it might go best with *habitat*.
Mrs. Gilpin:	Why do you think this page should be marked with *habitat*?
Doug:	Well, it means that's where cheetahs live.
Mrs. Gilpin:	Okay, now let's mark this page with a sticky note that says *habitat*. That way when you start taking notes you will know this page has information you might want to gather about where cheetahs live. Did you learn anything else on this page?
Doug:	Yes, it says that *cheetah* means "spotted one."
Mrs. Gilpin:	I didn't know that! Let's look at our chart again. What category might that fit into?
Doug:	[*Reads the chart*] I'm not sure. It's not *habitat*, or *food*, or *adaptations*.
Mrs. Gilpin:	You're right. It doesn't really seem to fit into any of our categories. But it is an interesting fact. Maybe we could add a category.
Doug:	Yeah, like "fun fact." I've seen those in some books.
Mrs. Gilpin:	Yes, I have too. That's a great idea. Let's be sure to share it with the class during sharing time.

Technology Tip

As students begin finding information related to the key questions, I begin posting threads on our class blog. Students can go to the class blog and respond to my questions, share their own thinking and learning with one another, and respond to what their peers have shared. This can be done while at home, in our computer lab, or on the classroom computers. It's another way for students to discuss and share their learning with each other. At first, my threads generally attempt to get students to share interesting facts they have found and to spur discussion among the students about what they're learning; see the sample thread below.

Sample discussion board thread:

My Post:	What is the most interesting thing you have learned about your animal so far?
Luke:	The most interesting thing I learned is the snowy owl lives in the arctic.
Hunter:	The most interesting thing I learned is giraffes have to spread their legs just to drink because of their long legs.
Marta:	Wow Hunter, I did not know that!
Lila:	Wow Luke that is cool!
Bella:	Dolphins can jump 3–4 feet high!
Marta:	Bella, what do dolphins eat?
Bella:	They eat a lot of fish.

I continue to use our class blog throughout the project as a place for students to share their learning, to answer higher-level questions, and to share with one another their thoughts and reflections about the project.

SHARING TIME

During this sharing time, I want Doug to share what we discussed in his conference.

Mrs. Gilpin:	So today we learned a little more about researching. We learned about how we can break down our larger topic into smaller ones to help guide our research and organize the information we are finding. Doug, while I was conferencing with you, you brought up a fact you found. Can you share that fact?
Doug:	I found out that *cheetah* means "spotted one."
Mrs. Gilpin:	Can you share with your classmates what we decided about that fact?
Doug:	We decided it didn't really fit into the topics on the chart so I didn't

know how to mark it. But it's really cool and I didn't know that. I want to include it in my project. So we decided it was an interesting fact, or kind of like a fun fact.

Mrs. Gilpin: Yes! When you are researching you might find a lot of facts that don't fit into one of our subtopics but you really like them and want to share that information, so I am going to add a new topic to our chart. I am going to write down, *Interesting facts/Fun facts*. Would anyone else like to share what they were working on today?

I allow several students to share.

Assessment for Step One: Narrow the Focus and Develop a Key Question

My main date of assessment for this part of the project comes from my conference notes. Through these notes, I am able to identify each student's strengths and challenges in going through the processes of topic selection and information gathering. I record my notes on the assessment checklist I have developed for the project; see page 121. This checklist could easily be adapted as a rubric.

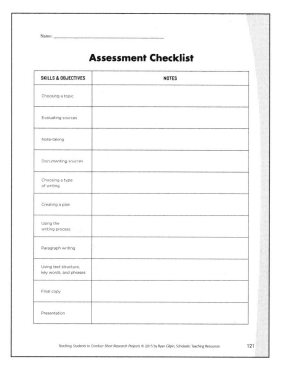

Teaching Students to Conduct Short Research Projects © 2015 by Ryan K. Gilpin, Scholastic Teaching Resources

Chapter 2

Conducting Research

Once my students have a better understanding of what research is and have chosen a topic, they are ready to begin the actual process of researching and gathering information to answer specific questions about their subject. At this point, I like to review the features of nonfiction with students because they'll be reading lots of nonfiction while they're researching—and also because they will be using these features in their own writing. I also take time during this stage to show students how to evaluate their sources, which helps them to become more efficient in gathering information. And I teach them to take notes so they don't forget the information they've learned and want to include in their projects. After they have finished gathering all of their information, I address the importance of documenting sources.

Chapter 2 Lessons

- Exploring Features of Nonfiction (1–3 Days)
- Evaluating Sources (1 Day)
- Note-Taking (2 Days)
- Documenting Sources (1 Day)

During this part of the project, I model researching my own topic. For this purpose, I choose a topic that no one has selected and find a set of books and materials I can use to model for each of the lessons. I continue to use these materials and the notes I take in this stage of the project to plan, write, and present my own research project.

Lesson 5: Exploring Features of Nonfiction (1–3 Days)

Before launching the first research project of the year, I will already have taught a unit on nonfiction reading, covering the features of nonfiction texts and how to read them to boost comprehension. Because conducting research involves reading a great amount of nonfiction, I often review nonfiction text features and reading strategies during the start of the project. I may repeat mini-lessons from my reading unit, meet with students individually, or conduct a few reading groups to help my students practice these skills.

The mini-lesson here reviews nonfiction features students had learned previously, and for this I pull out the chart we made during that unit. If you have not previously discussed features of nonfiction with your students, you may want to spend a day or two introducing them; see the list of feature and strategies I regularly teach in the box on page 31. It is also important to have plenty of reading material that is easy or just right for your students so that they can easily find information for their projects. I have put together a list of authors and series of books that are great for independent reading in grades 2–4; see page 31.

MATERIALS

- Chart of nonfiction text features
- Chart with categories from Lesson 4
- Books, magazines, and websites at various reading levels related to research topic
- Conferencing notebook
- Book with nonfiction features for modeling

Mini-Lesson

Mrs. Gilpin: Over the past few days we have been looking through books and magazines to start gathering information about our animals. The materials you have been reading are nonfiction. Nonfiction texts are very different from fictional texts, and we learned a lot about nonfiction texts few weeks ago. Can anyone remember a way that nonfiction is different from fiction?

Emelia: The information is real.

Luke: It's not made up.

Ana: The author is giving you facts.

Carter: The pages look different.

Mrs. Gilpin: Carter, let's think about that. The pages often look different in nonfiction books, though not always. What is one thing that you might see on the page of a nonfiction book that you might not in a fictional book?

Simon: Pictures?

Mrs. Gilpin: Yes, pictures might be one of those things. Anything else you might notice that you are reading?

Nonfiction Text Features and Reading Strategies

TEXT FEATURES

* *Headings*
* *Subheadings*
* *Photographs*
* *Illustrations*
* *Captions*
* *Table of Contents*
* *Glossary*
* *Index*
* *Maps*
* *Diagrams*
* *Fact Boxes or Fun Facts*
* *Bulleted Lists*
* *Sidebars*
* *Boldface Words*
* *Tables and Charts*
* *Graphs*

READING SKILLS/STRATEGIES

* *Determining important details and main idea*
* *Making inferences*
* *Using text structure to explore relationships among information, ideas, and events*

Nonfiction Authors and Series

FAVORITE NONFICTION AUTHORS

* *David Adler*
* *Melvin Berger*
* *Nic Bishop*
* *Matt Christopher*
* *Gail Gibbons*
* *Bobbie Kalman*
* *Mary Pope Osborne*
* *Seymour Simon*

FAVORITE NONFICTION SERIES AND MAGAZINES

* *DK Eye Wonder and DK Readers (DK Children)*
* *Gareth Stevens Vital Science Library (Gareth Stevens Publishing)*
* *I Am Biography Series (Scholastic)*
* *If You Lived Series (Scholastic)*
* *Kids Discover Magazines (Kids Discover)*
* *Let's-Read-and-Find-Out Science Series (Harper Collins Children's)*
* *National Geographic Kids Books and Magazines (National Geographic)*
* *The Life Cycle Series (Crabtree)*
* *Magic Tree House Fact Trackers (Random House Kids)*
* *Scholastic Biography Series (Scholastic)*
* *Scholastic First Biographies (Scholastic)*
* *Discover More (Scholastic)*
* *Q and A Series (Scholastic)*
* *Smart Words Reader (Scholastic)*
* *Straightforward Science Series (Scholastic)*
* *TIME for Kids Biographies (TIME for Kids)*
* *True Book Series (Scholastic)*
* *Who Was? Series (Penguin)*

Doug:	Captions with the pictures!
Phil:	Fun Facts!
Maria:	Headings!

My students are starting to remember a lot of the features we looked at in our reading unit, so this is when I pull up the chart "Features of Nonfiction" that we created during that unit.

Mrs. Gilpin	Yes, all of those things will be in the books and magazines you are reading. Do you remember what we call those?
Lisa:	Features?
Mrs. Gilpin	Yes, features. When we did our nonfiction reading unit we created this chart of all the features we noticed and how they helped us better understand nonfiction texts. These features can help you gather information. As you are researching your animal, if you come across one of these features, I want you to stop and use it to help you gather some information. Let's review a few before we go off to do our work today.

Features of Non Fiction
- Real Pictures
- Captions
- Heading
- Glossary
- Index
- Table of Contents
- Bold Words
- Bullets
- Illustrations
- Side bar
- Sub heading
- Diagram
- Timeline
- Fun facts

I review a few of the features using The Life Cycle of a Koala *by Bobbie Kalman. This is the mentor text I use throughout the project. The review helps to activate students' prior knowledge to help with their comprehension of the texts they are using for research.*

Mrs. Gilpin	I have a book here that I am going to look at with you. First, let's do a feature walk of this section. Remember, a feature walk is when you look at the pages to see what features there are. I'm looking at this page and I notice a heading, a picture, and a caption. I know that headings often get me thinking about what I am going to read about. For instance this says "Home on the Range." That gets me thinking before I even read the section that I am going to find out where a koala's home is.

I begin reading the section aloud. Once I'm done with the section, I go back to point out the pictures and captions.

Mrs. Gilpin	Now that I've read these two pages, I want to go back and look at the pictures and read the captions. They will often give me more information, and I don't want to miss out on something important.

As I read the captions, I make sure to emphasize that they did give me more information about my animal.

Mrs. Gilpin	I'm so glad I went back and read the captions. Although the paragraphs told me about a koala's home range, I didn't know that they will travel long distances to get back to their range if removed. From now on, whenever I am reading nonfiction, I will be sure to

stop and read the captions from pictures, too! Today as you are researching, make sure you pay attention to what features are on the pages. To help with this I am going to leave this chart up so that as you're reading you can access it to help you remember how to use those features as you come across them.

WORK TIME/CONFERENCING

Before sending students off to begin researching, I give them a quick reminder to use sticky notes to mark the subtopics we decided on the previous day.

Depending on how well the students did the day before with this task, I may do a quick modeling of marking pages with sticky notes to remind them how to do it. Otherwise, I check how well they are doing when I conference. While conferencing, I focus on reviewing nonfiction features, how well students are able to comprehend the information they're reading, and how well they're marking the information with the subtopic sticky notes. I conference with my struggling readers first so they get the support they need to find relevant information to complete this project.

Mrs. Gilpin: Hi, Carter! I'm so excited that you chose to research sharks! I have a really interesting book about sharks here and I want to look at it with you so we can gather more information for your project. Let's look at the first section together, and then you can read the rest of the book on your own. First let's do a feature walk of this section. When you look at these two pages, what features do you notice right away?

The book I'm using with this student is National Geographic Readers: Sharks!

Carter: Um, I see a heading and a picture . . . and the picture has a . . . [*He looks at the chart paper we reviewed during the mini-lesson*] a caption!

Mrs. Gilpin: Great! Let's think about these features. You see a heading. What do headings help us do?

Carter: [*Again he looks at the chart.*] They tell us what we might read about.

Mrs. Gilpin: Yes! They help get our brains thinking about what information we are about to read. I want you to read the heading and stop to think about and predict what information might be on this page.

Carter: It says "Shark Pups," and I think maybe it's about babies.

Mrs. Gilpin: So now you have a prediction about the kind of information you might find here. Read the two paragraphs on this page and stop. Then look at the other information on the page. Once you are done, mark this section with a sticky note and write what category the information on this page fits into.

After he finishes, I discuss with him the information he has gathered.

Mrs. Gilpin: So what was one thing you learned while reading this section?

Carter:	Baby sharks are called *pups*. And some pups grow in their mom but not all of them.
Mrs. Gilpin:	I see you put a sticky note with *life cycle* on it. What made you decide on that category?
Carter:	It's about babies and moms.
Mrs. Gilpin:	Let's look at the picture and caption. Did that give you more information about mother sharks and their babies?
Carter:	Kind of. It was about lemon sharks and fish that like them because they can eat their food.
Mrs. Gilpin:	That sounds interesting, and I think it might fit well with *food and diet* since it's about the lemon shark's food chain. Let's mark this page with another sticky note. I'm so glad you read that caption; otherwise we wouldn't have known there was information about food and diet on this page! It's important as we research to read everything on the page to help us find all the information the author of the book wanted us to know!

SHARING TIME

For sharing time in this lesson, I place students into groups of four or five. They then share with one another various features they found while reading and how these helped in gathering information. Then we have a whole-class discussion.

Mrs. Gilpin:	I'd like for us to take a moment and share which features we used and how they helped us to gather information about our animals. Carter, would you share with the class what we did together today?
Carter:	We were reading about shark pups. The picture on the page was about fish that eat leftovers from sharks. The caption helped me find *food and diet* facts in the section about shark babies.
Mrs. Gilpin:	That's right. When Carter and I were reading together we thought the page was only going to give us information about a shark's life cycle. When we read the caption we realized there was more information on the page! It's important to pay attention to features so you get all of the information the author wanted to share with you instead of just bits and pieces. Does anyone else want to share a feature they used and how it helped?.
Luke:	I was reading about owls today, and there was a word that was in bold. I didn't know what that word meant but I looked in the glossary and found out what it meant.
Mrs. Gilpin:	What word was that, Luke?
Luke:	*Strigidae.* It's the type of face an owl can have. It means it's a round face.
Mrs. Gilpin:	Wow, so you used the glossary to help understand a word you didn't know. The glossary is a great place to look up a word you don't know, and if a word is in boldface that means it's important to understand. You guys have done an amazing job researching your

animals over the past few days. You are using your knowledge of nonfiction features to help in understanding the materials you're reading and you're marking pages with the categories we're focusing on. Tomorrow we will begin note-taking so that you can begin creating plans for your projects. Remembering how you use these features to help you with your reading will really help you as you plan your writing.

Lesson 6: Evaluating Sources (1 Day)

Once we've discussed our theme and the subtopics students will be researching, I move on to how they can determine whether a given source will be useful or not. Although students have spent several days reading, they need to take time to determine whether or not the texts they have will be useful in their research. The two key questions I focus on with my third graders are: *Does this source have information related to the key questions or theme?* and *Is this text an appropriate reading level for me?* In my mini-lesson, I model how to use an index and a table of contents to find specific information and determine whether a book will have relevant information. While conferencing, I address the appropriateness of the reading level of sources and what students can do if the book doesn't have an index or table of contents. Even though I have gathered books and other materials for my students to read, I think it is important for them to decide for themselves which resources will be useful in researching their topic. This will help them find information more easily. In addition, they'll be reading material that is appropriate for them and that they can understand, which will make note-taking and synthesizing information less challenging.

Although this lesson doesn't ask students to evaluate how accurate the information is, how credible the authors may be, or whether a book is up to date with the information, these issues do come up in my conferences and during sharing time. This discernment is an important skill to teach, so I do cover it briefly with my students. By being encouraged to take the time to determine whether a book has enough information or not, students begin to realize that some books may be better than others. As students get older and are expected to evaluate sources at a higher level, these new, more challenging skills will come to them more easily because they are already in the habit of determining whether a book is going to be helpful or not.

MATERIALS

- Chart with theme and subtopics
- Nonfiction mentor text for modeling
- Books, magazines, and websites at various reading levels related to research topic
- Conferencing notebook

Mini-Lesson

I start by reminding students of the key questions and the subtopics they are researching. This gets them thinking and refreshes their memory of the specific information they will be looking for during this lesson. In this mini-lesson, I do a lot of talking in order to model for students how to use features of nonfiction to determine if a book has the information they need. Once I have reviewed the subtopics we're focusing on, I begin to discuss evaluating sources.

Mrs. Gilpin: You have gathered a lot of books and magazines about your topics and you have been studying your materials. When we are researching, not every resource is going to be helpful. To ensure that we are using the best resources for our purpose, we need to evaluate the sources we find. Today I am going to model for you how I can quickly and easily determine if a resource has the information I need for my project. I have a book here on koalas, and I'd like to know if it would be a good one to use for my research. I need a quick way to see if there is information in this book that might answer my questions.

Since we reviewed nonfiction features the day before, students are familiar with the index and table of contents, so modeling how to use them will be very helpful.

Mrs. Gilpin: When researching, we want to find information quickly. There are a few features of nonfiction that can quickly help me determine if a book has the exact information I'm looking for and where I can find it. Then I can do two things: decide if this book should be one I use to gather information, and, if so, know what pages I should read. The first thing I am going to do is look in the index. The index is at the back, or end, of the book and it has key words listed in alphabetical order.

I turn to the back of my book and show students the index.

Mrs. Gilpin: Next to the words there are numbers. These are the page numbers where I can find this information. The first subtopic I want to research is habitat. I know some key words for this topic are *habitat, home,* and *range*. As I look through the index I see the word *home*. I also see the word *range*. I know right away that this book has some information about my animal's habitat.

As I'm reading through the index, I hold the book up so students can see how the words are listed. I model looking up key words for two more of the subtopics students are researching before modeling using the table of contents.

Mrs. Gilpin: Now that I have looked through the index, I'm beginning to think this might be a helpful resource, but there is another place I can look in a book to find information quickly and determine if it will be a good resource. That is the table of contents. I will read the table of contents to see if there are any sections related to my categories.

I begin reading aloud the table of contents to my students.

Mrs. Gilpin: As I read I see "Life with Mom" and "Where Does a Koala Live?" so I'm thinking this book is really going to help me as I gather information. After looking at these two parts of the book I am thinking this is definitely going to be a resource that will help me complete my project.

Teaching Students to Conduct Short Research Projects © 2015 by Ryan K. Gilpin, Scholastic Teaching Resources

Now that I have modeled how to use the index and the table of contents, I discuss how to check whether the reading level of a resource is a good match.

Mrs. Gilpin: Another thing to think about as you're reading is whether or not the material feels like a comfortable reading level for you. When you are reading at a comfortable level, you can recall information easily or tell someone what you learned after reading without having to check information in the book.

I read one paragraph from my book aloud to my students. I close the book and retell what I have read.

Mrs. Gilpin: By taking the time to read a little of a book and retelling the information to someone, you will determine if the book will be a good resource for you to use. When reading, you want the book to be at your comfortable reading level so you can learn the information.

Finally, I introduce the task for the day.

Mrs. Gilpin: Today you are going to look at the sources you have and check the index and table of contents to help determine whether or not that source will be helpful in your research. Then I want you to read a little and see if the book is at your comfortable reading level. As you are working, you may also discover other ways to determine if a book is going to be a good resource. During sharing time we will talk about how we were able to determine if a source would be a useful one.

WORK TIME/CONFERENCING

My conferences for this lesson focus on three things:

- Helping students use the index and table of contents

- Helping students with books or other sources that don't have either of these features find alternative ways to determine if a source will be useful

- Helping students determine if the sources are at a comfortable reading level

The first conference is with a struggling reader. The student in the following conference was able to look through the index of his books and had decided they would be useful in gathering information; however, a few of them were well above his reading level. I did not want to tell him he couldn't use the books, but rather wanted to guide him to make that conclusion on his own. I approach it in such a way that he will not feel as though he is being told no, but rather will be making a good decision for himself. This also will increase the chance that, as he works independently, he will be able to decide for himself what is appropriate or not.

Mrs. Gilpin: All right, Greg, I want to look at your books with you because there is something else you want to do when researching. You want to make sure you are comfortable with what you're reading. Why do you think we want to be reading at a comfortable level instead of a challenging level when doing research?

Greg:	It might be, well, it would be too hard for me to read. I won't get any research done.
Mrs. Gilpin:	You're right. You want to make sure that when you are researching you understand what you are reading. This will help you gather more information. So you and I are going to look at a few of your books and you are going to decide if they are comfortable for you or maybe a bit challenging.

We begin to look through some of his books. I have him read the first few sentences in a one of them and then look through the pages. Once he has done this I have him decide whether or not he should use it for researching. He had trouble with quite a few of the words on the first page of the first book we looked at.

Mrs. Gilpin:	I want you to take a moment and think about what you just read. Was it easy to understand the information, or was it so challenging that you weren't sure what you were reading about?
Greg:	Well, I didn't know a lot of the words. And I'm not sure what this was [*points to word* species].
Mrs. Gilpin:	Do you think after reading those few sentences you could tell someone facts from that page?
Greg:	Probably not. It was hard.
Mrs. Gilpin:	Okay, so let's put this book aside and look at another one.

This time I give him a text that I know is at an appropriate reading level. After he reads a few sentences we talk about the difference between the two books. This leads him to decide what book would be better to use when researching.

Mrs. Gilpin:	Greg, we have just looked at two resources you have for you research. After looking at both, which one do you think would be a better resource for you to use?

He chooses the one that is at an appropriate reading level.

Mrs. Gilpin:	Why do you think you should use this one?
Greg:	Well, it was okay for me to read. I knew all of the words. I think I can tell someone about it too.

I check for his understanding of the text by having him read a passage.

Mrs. Gilpin:	What is a fact you would share after reading these sentences?
Greg:	Snakes use their senses to hunt.
Mrs. Gilpin:	Great, Greg! I think you're right; this would be a good book for you to use.
Greg:	[*He points to the more challenging book,*] That one—maybe they have the label things. Maybe I could read those?
Mrs. Gilpin:	You mean the captions and diagrams? You bring up a good point. Although this book is a little challenging, you might be able to use it.

Teaching Students to Conduct Short Research Projects © 2015 by Ryan K. Gilpin, Scholastic Teaching Resources

Absolutely you can look through the book at the pictures and other features and gather information. But this one [*the easier book*] would be best for you to read first when gathering your information. That way you get enough information from the comfortable books first and then go through the more challenging ones to get more information.

We continue to divide the stack of books he has into two piles, one with the books that he finds to be at his comfortable reading level and one with the books that are challenging. Then I have him begin looking at the index and table of contents of each of the easier books to determine if they will have enough information.

Mrs. Gilpin: Now that we have some books for you to read, I want you to take some time to look through each index and table of contents like I did in the mini-lesson. When I check back with you, I want you to share which books you think will be most helpful when you start taking notes.

In deciding on their own whether a book is or is not appropriate for them, students do not feel hindered in any way. It gives them further ownership of the project. It also allows them to practice a skill I want them to have—how to choose books at an appropriate level. I was impressed that Greg knew that even if books were a bit too challenging they could still be helpful in some way. If I had just told him he couldn't read them he would have never figured out that although the text was too difficult, some of the text features were not.

As students begin the task of looking through the index and table of contents in each of their books, they begin to realize some of their books do not have these features. As a result, quite a few of my conferences during this lesson focus on how else students can determine whether the books would be helpful or not.

Eliza: Mrs. Gilpin, this book doesn't have a table of contents or an index. I'm not sure what to do.

Mrs. Gilpin: Let's take a look at this book. What could you do with this book to see if it is going to have the information?

Eliza: Well, I could look through it. It doesn't have a lot of words; it has a lot of pictures. Could I just read it?

Mrs. Gilpin: Absolutely. You can go through and look at it, read some of the features and then decide if this might be a good one to use. I would like for you to do that, and I'll come back later to see what you decided.

I conference with a few other students, allowing Eliza time to explore the book. When I return we discuss her decision.

Mrs. Gilpin: Eliza, what did you decide about this book after taking some time to look through and read it?

Eliza: I think it might be helpful. It had a diagram and pictures of their homes. I also read a caption about gathering food. I want to use it.

Another student had the same concern, but she had a very good approach for figuring out if it would be a good book to use. She realized that the author had written many other nonfiction books, and because of that she felt she trusted the author. This is something we explore further as a class during various author studies throughout the year. It can also be another mini-lesson while researching.

Aubrey:	This book didn't have an index or table of contents. But it's by Gail Gibbons. I think I've read other books by her, and I think she does a good job with stuff.
Mrs. Gilpin:	Aubrey, you're right. Gail Gibbons writes a lot of nonfiction books, and although it doesn't have a table of contents or index, we can guess that this book would be helpful because she wrote it.
Aubrey:	I'll probably just read it because it isn't long and it looks like it has a lot of facts. I can tell it has a bunch of information because there are diagrams and pictures.

The following conference is with a student who had a book with an index but who was having difficulties determining which subtopics words in the index matched. Together we went through the words to determine whether the book would be a good source for her. As we conferenced, we referred back to the chart with the theme and subtopics listed.

Katy:	I couldn't see how these [*she points to words in the index*] would fit with what's on there [*she points to the chart with subtopics*]. Like the word *air*—it would be something with *survival* for dolphins.
Mrs. Gilpin:	Yes, *air* would be important because dolphins need air to do what?
Katy:	Well, it would be in *adaptations*, to breathe.
Mrs. Gilpin:	Okay, let's look at a few other words. What about the word *hunt*?
Katy:	Probably *food and diet*. Oh, and the words *catch together* would probably be *life cycle* since dolphins stay together.
Mrs. Gilpin:	I think you are beginning to see how you can use these words to determine what subtopic they fit with and whether this book would have enough information.
Katy:	I think this book is good to use. It actually has a lot of words.

SHARING TIME

During sharing time I review with students some of things that came up while conferencing. I have a few students share what they did when concerns arose. By sharing these concerns everyone will hear and learn about the strategies we discussed in the mini-lesson and some new strategies to use when evaluating sources.

Mrs. Gilpin:	During writing workshop today I asked you to go through your books to determine whether or not they are going to be helpful in your research. In the mini-lesson we discussed how some books or resources might be better than others. I modeled for you how you can check in the index and table of contents to find out if books had enough information or not to be helpful in your research. What did you find as you were doing this today?
Lea:	I found a book that will be helpful with my research. It didn't have an index though.

Mrs. Gilpin:	Quite a few of you were concerned in conferences that your books didn't have the features I modeled. Aubrey, can you share with the class what you did when you realized your book didn't have these features?
Aubrey:	We quickly looked through the book at some of the features and decided if it would be a good book or not.
Mrs. Gilpin:	Yes, exactly. Aubrey, what else helped us decide on one of your books?
Aubrey:	Well one of the books was by Gail Gibbons, and I know she wrote other books I've read. Her books always have good information, and they are always nonfiction.
Mrs. Gilpin:	Yes, we looked at who the author was and realized she writes a lot of nonfiction books for kids. We decided that even though her book didn't have an index or table of contents, it would be a good choice. We could trust that her information would be helpful because she is a nonfiction author and has written other great nonfiction books. One way to determine if a book will be a good resource is to check and see who the author is, or check to see if you are familiar with the author's work. If you know who the author is or know the series has other books you've read, you can tell if the book would be helpful in your research.
Katy:	Like the Magic Tree House books. They have really good information, and I know there is one on dolphins. That might help me!
Mrs. Gilpin:	Good thinking, Katy! Some of you decided that a few of your books without indexes would be good resources, but that you might use the books with an index first when you begin taking notes. Why was that?
Evelyn:	Because you can find stuff easier and faster.
Pam:	Because you know exactly where it is. You don't have to keep flipping through pages.
Mrs. Gilpin:	Yes. When you use an index or the table of contents it helps you find the exact information you are looking for and you can find it a lot quicker than if you were trying to read the book cover to cover. That doesn't mean the other books won't be helpful. It just means you might want to start with the books that do have an index or table of contents. Then when you are finished using those books you can read the ones without those features.

Now, there is one more thing I conferenced with some of you about that will help when determining if a book is a good resource. When you are researching, you want to make sure the books you are reading are at a comfortable reading level. Why is that important when researching? |
| **Evelyn:** | If you choose a really hard book, you can't really read it. |
| **Lea:** | You won't be learning. |

Noah:	Yeah. You wouldn't get any information.
Greg:	Because you don't understand it.
Mrs. Gilpin:	If your book is easy or just right, what will you be able to do?
Lea:	You will learn more about your animal, because you understand it!
Pam:	If it's a hard book, probably it will have hard words and you won't know what they mean.
Mrs. Gilpin:	Yes, so another good way to determine if a book will be a good resource is asking yourself, "Can I read and understand this?" Usually by reading one page or one paragraph you will be able to answer that question. There are going to be some books that have a lot of really good information, but if you can't understand it will you be able to take notes or gather information from that book? Probably not! And that's okay. There a lot of really good resources for you to use that are at a good reading level for you! As you learn more about your topic, you may be able to use a more challenging text because you'll have more background knowledge about your animal and a better understanding of the vocabulary associated with your topic.

I sum up the key points I want children to think about when evaluating sources.

Mrs. Gilpin:	When evaluating your sources, there are a few things to think about: Can I read and understand this material easily? Can I paraphrase or retell what I have learned? Am I familiar with this author or series? Does this author know a lot about this topic? Does the index or table of contents have words or phrases that fit with the specific information I'm looking for? Will this text have what I need?

Teaching Tip

My students also have access to digital sources, but because of their age I typically preselect the websites they can access for information. During this project, I teach a lesson about evaluating digital sources using a framework devised by Nell K. Duke called WWWDOT:

W—Who wrote this and what credentials do they have?

W—Why was it written?

W—When was it written?

D—Does it help meet my needs?

O—Organization of the site?

T—To-do list for the future (i.e. corroborate the information with other websites)

Working in small groups, and using the websites I've preselected, students and I go through a list of questions to determine whether each website would be a good one. For more on WWWDOT, check out "The WWWDOT Approach to Improving Students' Critical Evaluation of Websites" (Zhang, Duke, Jiménez, 2011).

Teaching Students to Conduct Short Research Projects © 2015 by Ryan K. Gilpin, Scholastic Teaching Resources

As I review these things I write them on chart paper as a reference for the class to use later.

Mrs. Gilpin: Good job today, class! Now that you have a better idea of how to determine whether a text will be a helpful resource, you're ready to start taking notes!

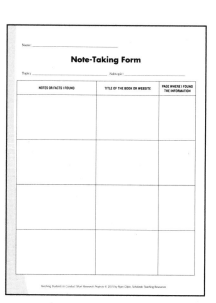

Evaluating Sources
1. Can I read and understand this material easily?
2. Can I paraphrase or retell what I have read?
3. Am I familiar with this author or series?
4. Does this author know a lot about this topic?
5. Will this text have the information I need?

Lesson 7: Note-Taking (2 Days)

Note-taking is an important skill for students to learn because it helps them paraphrase what they have read, organize their information in a meaningful way, and understand the importance of documenting their sources. It also helps students remember important information they want to include in their projects. To help them remember and process new information, I often give them the opportunity to share their research orally with a partner before writing the notes. This extra step is invaluable for helping students make the information their own, and it's especially beneficial for English language learners because it gives them extra practice with vocabulary.

I usually model note-taking two or more times for students as a mini-lesson, and also work with students who are having trouble with this skill one-on-one or in small groups. I have provided a sample of the note-taking form I give students (page 122). I have also had students use large index cards, making sure that they label each card with one of their subtopics, or even regular notebook paper.

MATERIALS

- Chart paper and marker
- Note-Taking Form (p. 122) or large index cards, several per student
- Mentor text for modeling
- Books, magazines, and websites at various reading levels related to research topic
- Conferencing notebook

Mini-Lesson

I start this mini-lesson by reviewing the subtopics we have chosen to research and by asking students to remind themselves what they have been doing with the sticky notes while reading about their topic. Then I do a modeled note-taking lesson.

Mrs. Gilpin: Today I am going to model for you what proper note-taking looks like. First, I'm going to get everything I need: my book, my note-taking forms for each of my subtopics, and a pencil. Notice how I've written a subtopic on each sheet. This way I can collect information from several sources on the same subtopic in one place. Now I'm going to read aloud to you from my koala book. The first thing I'm going to do is find a page where I placed a sticky note. Here, on the first two pages I notice I wrote *habitat*, so I'm going to take out my note-taking form that has *habitat* as the topic. This way when I'm done reading I can write down what I learned.

As I read, I think aloud about the various features on the page to remind students to read everything on the page. I also stop after each section to review and paraphrase what I just read. When I have completed the two pages I explain to students that I will model how to take notes, emphasizing that it's important not to copy directly from the book but rather to use my own words. I also explain that notes do not need to be full sentences; I can just write key words or phrases.

Mrs. Gilpin: I have just finished reading these two pages and I'm ready to take notes. I don't want to copy what the author has written because those are not my own words. I want to make sure I write what I have learned using my own words by paraphrasing or summarizing what I just read. To help make sure I don't copy sentences from the book, I'll close it while I write my notes.

I close the book and set it aside to begin taking notes.

Mrs. Gilpin: I'm going to think aloud here, but when you're working on your own, it can be a big help to talk with a partner about your reading before writing your notes. That helps you remember the information better and makes it easier to put it in your own words. When reading these two pages I learned that koalas are found in Australia, so I'm going to write "Australia" on my paper. I also learned that they live in eucalyptus trees, so I'm going to write that fact down too. I remember that they are found in three states, but I can't remember their names, so I'm going to need to look at that page again. I am not going to copy the sentences the author wrote, but I will write down the names of those three states.

After looking at the page, I write down the three states on my note-taking form. I then ask students to think about what I did.

Mrs. Gilpin: Can anyone share what they noticed I did to take these notes?

After one or two students share what they noticed, I model how to keep track of where I am finding this information about my animal. On my note-taking forms, there's a place to write the title and page number where each piece of information was found. This helps students understand the importance of documenting where they find their information. It also enables us to go back and check to make sure we haven't copied directly from the book—and while I'm at it, I can ensure that students have interpreted the information correctly.

Mrs. Gilpin: Now that I have some really good information about where koalas live, I need to document it. I'm going to write down the title of the

Teaching Students to Conduct Short Research Projects © 2015 by Ryan K. Gilpin, Scholastic Teaching Resources

book and the page number where I found this information. This is important because I will need to give credit to this author in my bibliography when I have finished my project.

I model where to write this information on the note-taking form. Once I'm done with the note-taking form, I summarize note-taking to the class. As I summarize, I write down the steps on chart paper.

| Mrs. Gilpin: | When taking notes, it's important to remember a few things. The first thing I want to do is read over the information. Then I want to close my book or put it down and get my note-taking form out. I then retell what I've read, either to myself or a friend. After that, I write down one fact at a time. These do not need to be in complete sentences; I can use key words or ideas. I also want to make sure that I am not copying directly from the book, and that is why I put it away while I write my facts down. Once I have the facts written down I make sure to document my source by writing the title of the book and the page number where I found this information. Today this is what you |

will be working on during your research time. If you are unsure of what to do, I will be around to conference, and you can check this chart as well.

Steps For Taking Notes
- Read through the text
- Close the text
- Think about what you read
- Retell what you read to yourself or a friend
- Write what you learned
- Document source
★ Never Copy from a text ★

WORK TIME/CONFERENCING

For this lesson, my conferences focus on helping students find information, interpret the information correctly, and write about it in their own words without copying from the texts. Below I share three note-taking conferences, each showcasing a common difficulty: organizing information, writing in their own words, and finding enough information.

Mrs. Gilpin:	Hi, Doug. Can you share with me some of the notes you've taken about cheetahs?
Doug:	Well, uh, I guess I don't have any.
Mrs. Gilpin:	Are you having trouble finding information?
Doug:	Not really. I've learned a lot about cheetahs—they live in Africa, they run really fast, they have cubs that stay with their moms. They have a line on their face that helps keep sun out of their eyes.
Mrs. Gilpin:	Wow! You really have learned a lot about cheetahs. Let's look in one book you read and find some of this information so you can start taking notes. As I look through this book I notice you marked pages with the category sticky notes. The heading on this page says "Living in Africa." I'd like for you to read the paragraph and then we will discuss it.

After giving him a moment to read the information and look at the map and picture, I ask him to tell me what he just learned.

Doug:	Cheetahs live in Africa.
Mrs. Gilpin:	Great! So let's write that down. Which note-taking form should we use?
Doug:	*Habitat.*
Mrs. Gilpin:	Was there any other information about their habitat?
Doug:	Well, they live in the savanna, which has lots of grass.
Mrs. Gilpin:	Okay, great. Let's write that down too.

Once he writes the notes, we then document the source, I have him read the next page he had marked with a sticky note, and we go through the same process again. Through conferencing, I realize Doug had read so much information and learned so much about cheetahs that he had become overwhelmed by the enormity of it all and was struggling to organize his thoughts. After we write down some facts together, he is able to complete the rest of his note-taking with very little assistance from me. Walking him through the process of taking notes during our conference allows him to succeed at this task. This next conversation is with a student who had copied from the book.

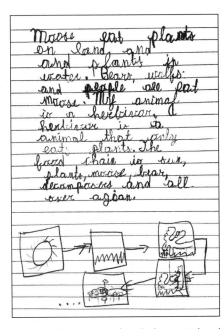

A student's notes on beavers

Mrs. Gilpin:	Hi, Liza. Can you share with me some of your notes on giraffes?
Liza:	Sure! I was looking at my book and where I found this information about giraffes eating.

When she shows me her notes I realize they were copied directly from the text.

Mrs. Gilpin:	Can you explain to me how you are taking notes?
Liza:	I'm reading it and then writing it down.
Mrs. Gilpin:	I want you to think about the mini-lesson today and how I was taking notes. Did I copy directly from the book, or did I find my own words when I wrote down the information?
Liza:	You used your own words.
Mrs. Gilpin:	Yes! What have you been doing when you are writing down your notes?
Liza:	I guess I copied it.

A student's notes, taken in her notebook

Teaching Students to Conduct Short Research Projects © 2015 by Ryan K. Gilpin, Scholastic Teaching Resources

Mrs. Gilpin:	Okay, let's try to use your own words. It's important that we not copy because that is someone else's work and we want this project to be our own. We will give credit to the author in our bibliography, but it's important that we find our own words to present the information we have learned. I want you to read this section again and close the book. Then we will talk about what you leaned.

As she's reading, I read the section as well. When she closes the book I ask her to tell me a few facts she learned.

Liza:	Giraffes eat for 12 hours a day and they eat 140 pounds of food a day. They use their tongues and they stretch them out to find food. The tongue pulls the leaves off of the tree.
Mrs. Gilpin:	Now I want you to take a minute and write each of those facts onto your *food and diet* note-taking forms. Once you are done with your notes I want you to document your source and then continue reading. I will check back with you to see how it's going.

Teaching Tip

If students are having difficulty finding information in a category, give them two to four specific questions to focus their search.

When I conferenced with Lisa, I quickly realized she was struggling to find her own words for her notes, but when she explained the information to me verbally she was able to easily paraphrase what she'd read. For some students, it's easier to discuss what they read with someone before writing it down; therefore, I allow time during our work time for students to explain to me and their peers what they've learned. This usually helps them write their notes.

This next conversation is with a student who found information about most of his subtopics, but was struggling to find enough information about one of them.

Mrs. Gilpin:	Hi, Beau. I'm noticing you have a lot of notes on your *habitat* and *food and diet* forms, but don't have much for *appearance*. Are you having trouble finding information?
Beau:	Kind of, but I don't really know what I should be looking for.
Mrs. Gilpin:	What kinds of things might fit with appearance?
Beau:	What they look like.
Mrs. Gilpin:	Yes! It might also include their size, weight, and the differences between males and females. I'm going to write a few questions down for you and then you can go and try to find the answers.

Some of the questions I write down for him to answer are: How big can male and female warthogs get? How much can they weigh? What colors are they?

SHARING TIME

Mrs. Gilpin:	Today you were busy taking notes. Can anyone share what was easy about taking notes?

Aubrey:	We had pages marked with our subtopics. I found *habitat* stuff about beavers and wrote it down.
Luke:	Yeah, it was easy to find what I was looking for since we marked pages with sticky notes.
Annette:	I found my turtle's food fast since I marked it yesterday.
Mrs. Gilpin:	Okay, so I'm hearing that you had an easy time finding what to write down because you marked pages using sticky notes with your subtopics. Can anyone share what was difficult or challenging about note-taking?
Liza:	It was really hard not to copy it from my book.
Phil:	It's hard to make my own words—closing the book and just writing it was a little easier. I don't want to copy. It's not mine.
Mrs. Gilpin:	Sometimes it can be really difficult to find your own way of writing information down, but try to remember that the authors of the books we are reading worked really hard and it wouldn't be fair to copy what they wrote. Plus, you want your writing to be your own! Doing a lot of reading and getting to know your topic, then trying to write down key words or phrases related to the information will help you to write it in your own words. We will continue to practice using our own words while taking notes again tomorrow, and we will be meeting in small groups so I can help you do that.

Learning to paraphrase rather than copy from their sources is one of the biggest challenges students face when learning to conduct research. By having them provide the page numbers where they found specific information, I can then go through and check to make sure they have not copied directly from texts or websites. I also have them do some writing for me in the evenings. Each day that they are researching and taking notes, I give them a writing assignment for homework. I ask them to write everything they know about their animal in relation to one of the categories we are researching—*habitat, food and diet, life cycle, adaptations, appearance,* and *threats.* This way they are writing what they have learned so far, without their sources in front of them (Duke & Bennett-Armistead, 2003, pp. 147–148). These writing pieces are also notes for them to reference when they begin writing their reports.

Lesson 8: Documenting Sources (1 Day)

Once students feel they have gathered enough information, I have them create a bibliography listing all sources, both print and digital, that they used while researching. I do this before they begin writing their drafts so they'll easily be able to find their sources if they need to clarify anything later. Students should learn early that documenting where they found their information is part of researching. I have provided a sheet (page 123) to help students create a bibliography, but students could also create a list in their writing journals or on a computer.

Teaching Students to Conduct Short Research Projects © 2015 by Ryan K. Gilpin, Scholastic Teaching Resources

MATERIALS

- Chart paper and marker
- Bibliography handout (page 123), one per student
- Books and materials students are using for research
- Conferencing notebook

Mini-Lesson

Mrs. Gilpin: We have been working hard at gathering information and facts about our animals, and we have used a lot of different sources. You have read many books, magazines, and websites to gather information. Today we are going to document all of the sources we have used while researching. On your note-taking forms, I asked you to write down the title of each book, magazine, or website you used. When researching it is very important that you document the sources you used so that others know where you found your information. This gives credit to other researchers and allows for those reading your work to find more information if they need it. In nonfiction books you often see a page at the very end that has other titles and websites listed. This is called a *bibliography* and that is what we are going to work on today.

At this point I show the students one of the books we used and its bibliography.

Mrs. Gilpin: I used quite a few books to gather my information about koalas so I am going to start a list. On this list I am going to include the title of the book and the author or authors of the book. If there isn't an author listed on the cover, I can look at the title page to see if it is mentioned there. If I can't find an author listed but I know the book is part of a series, I will write the name of the series here.

I model writing the title and author of one of my books on my chart paper.

Mrs. Gilpin: Today I am going to give you a sheet in which to list your resources. It has sections for books, magazines, and websites. If you watched a video, you can include that in the section with websites, since it was online.

WORK TIME/CONFERENCING

During their work time, students gather all the resources they used and begin writing down the information on the sheet I provided. They also have access to in-class computers so that they can document the websites they used. As they are working I go around the room to answer any questions they may have. The following conferences address two things that often come up while students work on this task: how to find an author's name when it isn't listed on the cover and what to do about a resource they read but did not take notes from. Many times students will leave titles of books off their list if they cannot find an author's name or if they only read a book. I address these two concerns in conferences because students need to understand the importance of documenting all of the sources they used when researching.

Pam: Mrs. Gilpin, I am having trouble finding the name of the author for this book. I don't think it has one.

Mrs. Gilpin: Let's take a look. I can see that the cover has a title and a publisher but you're right—I don't see the name of an author. When this happens I usually look at the title page. Sometimes the author or authors are listed there. Take a look!

Pam: [*She looks at the title page.*] Oh I see it now; it's right here. Now I can add this to my list.

Another student is looking at an encyclopedia of animals that does not have an author listed on the cover or title page.

Aubrey: Mrs. Gilpin, I'm looking and looking but don't see an author anywhere.

Mrs. Gilpin: Where have you looked?

Aubrey: I looked at the cover and title page, I looked in the back, and I can't find it.

Mrs. Gilpin: Let's look at the copyright page. Sometimes in big books like this encyclopedia there isn't an author but rather an editor instead. This is someone who helps put the book together. Let's look to see if that is the case with this book.

Together we look at the copyright page.

Aubrey: Would this be it? [*She points to "project editors."*]

Mrs. Gilpin: That's it. Now we can write that down in your bibliography.

This next conference is with a student who has read a book but doesn't use it when taking notes.

Beth: I read this one but I didn't use it when I was taking notes. Do I have to write that down too?

Mrs. Gilpin: Yes! Even if you didn't take notes when reading the book, you used that as a way to gather information while researching. You want to be sure to give credit so that that author is recognized for their work. Also, if someone reading your work wants to learn more about your topic, they can look at this list and see what other books or materials are available.

SHARING TIME

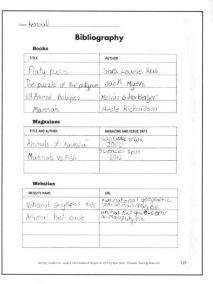

Completed bibliography

Mrs. Gilpin: Today I had you complete a bibliography of all the sources you used while researching. Why is it important to document these sources?

Pam: Well, we want to make sure that we share with others where we found the information we have.

Liam: Yeah, we can't copy from them.

Mrs. Gilpin: Yes! We want to make sure we give credit to others whose research we read or use while conducting our own research. What's another reason we want to document our sources?

Aubrey: So the people who read our books will know where to find other information.

Beth: Yeah, even if we don't take notes from a book, we should include it in our bibliography so that our readers know about it. Then they can look at it if they want more information.

Mrs. Gilpin: Yes. When we share our publications, someone might want to find more information and our bibliography will tell them where they can go and find it. Great job today, Third Grade! Now that we have chosen our topic and conducted our research we are ready to start planning our publications and do our writing!

Assessment for Step Two: Conduct the Research

For this part of the project I assess two areas:

- *Evaluating sources:* I take anecdotal notes in my conferencing notebook to document how well each student selects sources that he or she can comfortably use for research.

- *Note-taking:* I review students' note-taking forms to determine how well they are able to organize their notes by subtopic, whether they paraphrase or copy directly from texts, and whether they document their sources properly.

I record my notes about each of these areas on my assessment checklist for each student; see page 121.

Creating a Plan

After students have collected information about their topics, they move on to the next step of the project: planning their written piece, whether that's a poster, book, editorial, museum artifact description, or some other type of nonfiction text. The mini-lessons in this chapter focus on the planning part of the writing process. It's important for students to understand that writing is a process and that perhaps the most important part of this process is planning. For this stage of the research project, students begin by choosing what type of piece they want to create from a set of options I provide. They then create a plan for how they are going to organize their information and their writing. I have found that using a storyboard allows each student to decide what each page or section of their final product will include, where specific information will go, and which features of nonfiction they want to use. This format allows for creativity, enables students to use what they know about nonfiction writing, and helps them visualize what their final piece will look like.

Planning helps ensure that they will complete the project to its fullest without omitting any details they wanted to include. Students can then move on to writing their drafts with confidence, revise and edit their work, and ultimately publish a piece they're incredibly proud of. When they've published their work, they often recognize the importance of the plan they created and how it helped them throughout the writing process. Without it, they wouldn't have known where to begin or where to go once they started.

MAKING IT YOUR OWN

Depending on your students' needs and goals, as well as your own curricular objectives, you can provide various options for publication formats and planning tools. For the animal research unit, I give students the choice of creating a book, poster, brochure, or magazine. For other projects, students have created museum displays, speeches, feature articles—there are so many options to choose from! Of course, the type of planning tool you select will depend on the publication format. Remember to choose how you want your students to plan their writing before you begin these lessons. The main purpose of the plan is to provide guidance to your students as they begin to turn their notes into writing. In addition to storyboarding, you might have students complete a graphic organizer, outline, or sketch, or use any appropriate tool, always providing examples and modeling.

Chapter 3 Lessons

- Exploring Types of Nonfiction Publications (2 Days)
- Choosing What Type of Piece to Publish (1–2 Days)
- Creating a Plan (2 Days)

Lesson 9: Exploring Types of Nonfiction Publications (2 Days)

While students finish up their note-taking, I present mini-lessons on how to complete the actual project. This lesson spurs students to think about how they want to present the information they've collected. By looking at various types of nonfiction texts, they begin to consider how their information might be best organized and presented to their readers and what features of nonfiction they want to use. I like for this lesson to be an exploratory one for students, rather than my telling them about different types of texts and how information can be organized. When exploring on their own they often notice things that I might not necessarily have covered. Of course, the examples you share should match the options you're giving students for their final products.

For the animal research unit, I have a station with magazines, a station with posters, a station with brochures, and a few stations with books. I set up book stations using series that students enjoy reading. I do it this way because students are familiar with these books, enjoy them, and are likely to find them helpful as mentor texts when they begin planning their own books. I set up the stations at tables around the room. Each station has three or four examples of that particular type of nonfiction text. I make sure my examples clearly demonstrate that type of nonfiction. Giving students as much choice as possible in these texts allows for more creativity in the production of their own writing.

This lesson typically requires two days. You can set up all the stations on the first day and have students explore them all and then have them share their observations over two days (as I've done in the model lesson below), or you can set up half of the stations the first day and the other half the second day. I've done this lesson both ways and found both to be effective.

MATERIALS

- Examples of various types of nonfiction texts
- Chart paper and markers; prepare charts by writing the name of each station at the top of its own sheet
- Students' writing journals or other paper
- Conferencing notebook

Mini-Lesson

I begin this lesson by reviewing our chart that lists the tools for research. I do this because many of the tools students listed are types of nonfiction texts. After reviewing this list, I move into the next part of the lesson.

Mrs. Gilpin: Now that you're finishing up your research and note-taking, it's time to start thinking about the next step with this project: choosing the type of text you want to create and planning it. To help with this I've gathered many different types of nonfiction to share with you today. We're going to look at these and notice the different ways information can be organized. Then you'll begin thinking about how you want to present your information.

I show them a few examples by holding up different types of nonfiction. I usually show a poster, a magazine, a book, and a brochure, explaining and describing each. I then explain to students the activity they will be doing.

Mrs. Gilpin: Let's take a look at my collection here. I've got posters, books, magazines, and brochures. Each one of these has a lot of information about a particular subject but presents that information differently. I have set up stations around the room for you to explore. Each station has one type of nonfiction. You will be looking through these and writing down things you notice about them in your writing journals. Once everyone has gone through the stations, we will gather and discuss the observations you made about how the information was organized.

I show students the charts we will use to collect our observations about each type of nonfiction text.

Mrs. Gilpin: As you visit each station I want you to write down one or two things you notice right away when you look at the text. For example, when I open my book I can see right away that there are paragraphs along with small pictures. As you look through the various texts, you might notice features of nonfiction right away, and I want you to really take a look at how the pages are laid out. Instead of reading these texts to learn new information, I want you to focus on looking at how the author has taken the information and put it on the page.

I model writing my observations on the chart.

Mrs. Gilpin: Record your observations just like I do here. One of the stations you will visit has quite a few books from Bobbie Kalman's Life Cycle series. Since my koala book is a part of that series, I'll write one of my observations on this area of my chart. I noticed that there were paragraphs and pictures with captions, so that is what I'll write as an observation.

WORK TIME/CONFERENCING

I divide the class into groups and tell students they will have about five minutes at each station. I then send students to the various stations. As students rotate, I go to each station to ask questions about their observations. My conferences focus on what students are noticing about these texts in order to prepare them for planning their pieces. If they are familiar with the qualities that a particular type has, it will be easier for them to plan their own project. The following conference is with two students who are visiting a station with question-and-answer (Q&A) books.

Mrs. Gilpin:	Hi, Pam. Hi, Lea. Can you share with me what you're noticing about these books?
Pam:	What I learned is that they have a lot of words and then sort of like a small picture.
Mrs. Gilpin:	I'm noticing that, too! What have you noticed about how each page has started?
Pam:	Each page starts with a question.
Mrs. Gilpin:	Yes, I can see it starts with a question. That's a good observation; let's write that down.

I give students time to write, then ask another question.

Mrs. Gilpin:	Pam says each page starts with a question. What else do you notice about the page?
Lea:	It tells you the answer to the question.
Mrs. Gilpin:	How is it answering the questions?
Lea:	With a lot of writing. It has illustrations, but not captions or features.
Mrs. Gilpin:	These are great observations about Q&A books. A lot of times these books just have a question, an answer, and a picture. That's something to think about if you choose to publish a Q&A book.

I move on to conference with two students visiting the magazine station.

Mrs. Gilpin:	What have you noticed about magazines, Noah and Emily?
Noah:	They have a lot of words and writing, but they also have a lot of pictures. So it's not boring. It's fun to look at, but it has a lot of information. It's colorful!
Emily:	There are lots of things that are happening right now like in this year. Information about now, like in our world right now.
Noah:	They also have games, like puzzles.
Emily:	And comics.
Mrs. Gilpin:	These are all really good observations about magazines, so I want you to take a moment and write them in your notebook.

I give them a moment to write these observations down and then continue to conference.

Mrs. Gilpin: Magazines are a little different because they often have a lot of writing and pictures, but also a lot of other features as well, like comics or games. They are also often more current in their information since they are published periodically. When we gather with the class to discuss what we noticed, I want you to share these observations with your classmates!

The next group I visit with is the station with National Geographic Everything books. My students love reading these books, and many of them choose these books as their mentor texts when designing their own books.

Students at the magazine station

Mrs. Gilpin: Hi, Liam. I overheard you sharing with Evan an observation you made. Can you share that observation with me?

Liam: I realized that some of the pages are just pictures and don't have as many words, and some pages have more words than pictures. There are facts here—they separate them into boxes. That's what I found.

Mrs. Gilpin: It looks like you found some interesting things about how the books in this series are set up. Let's write these observations down—that way you will remember them when we gather to share.

I continue around the room having this sort of conversation at each station. Once all of the students have visited each station, we gather to discuss what they noticed. As they share their observations, I write them on my chart so we have a reference when planning our pieces.

SHARING TIME: DAY ONE

For sharing time, students bring with them the notes they took when visiting the stations. This helps them remember their observations and prepares them to share during our group discussion.

Mrs. Gilpin: As I rotated through the stations and had the opportunity to discuss with you what you were observing, I heard some great things! Now it's time for us to share with one another those observations. As you share, I will write down your observations for each station we had in the room. Today we are going to share what we noticed about magazines and brochures. Let's start with brochures. What are some things you noticed when at that station?

As students share I write down their observations on my chart and clarify or paraphrase what they have shared.

Aubrey:	Brochures were folded into parts.
Mrs. Gilpin:	Okay, so you saw that most brochures are folded into three parts; we call that a tri-fold.
Bill:	The cover was the title.
Noah:	Yeah, it was a picture with the name of the place.
Mrs. Gilpin:	I'm going to write on our chart here that the front introduced the topic, much like the cover of a book. Anything else you noticed?
Eliza:	It had a lot of colorful pictures, and writing with subheadings.
Mary:	And where to go, and phone numbers and stuff.
Mrs. Gilpin:	Yes, they did have a lot of colorful pictures and usually the text in a brochure has subheadings. Mary, what a great observation about the contact information and maps. I'm going to write these things down as well.

Once I have written down the information students shared about brochures, I review each detail with them.

Mrs. Gilpin:	Now I'd like for us to think about magazines. What were some things you noticed when at that station?
Emily:	The topics were things going on in the world, right now.
Mrs. Gilpin:	Yes, often magazines will focus on current topics that are important in society right now.
Evan:	Well, I did notice that there were stories about different things.
Pam:	And puzzles, fun stuff, games.
Evelyn:	Lots of pictures.
Greg:	And comics. I love those.
Mrs. Gilpin:	We've noticed many different things about magazines. We noticed that many times they can be related to current topics, they can have many articles with a lot of pictures, they can also have some fun activities like games and puzzles, and they can have comics.

What a great job everyone did today looking at the different kinds of nonfiction texts! Tomorrow we will finish sharing our observations about the posters and book series we looked at. Then you will begin thinking about what type of publication you would like to create and begin making a plan for it! |

Magazine Observations
- Current events   - lots of pictures
- Stories   - Articles   - Fun Facts
- Puzzles   - Comics
- Colorful

SHARING: DAY TWO

On the second day, students share what they noticed about the rest of the texts they explored. After I've written down all the information they've gathered, I explain why I did this lesson with them. This helps them understand how looking at these texts will relate to their own work.

> **Mrs. Gilpin:** The reason I wanted to go over this with you is because soon you are going to write your own nonfiction pieces. You'll get to choose what type of text you want write to share information about your animal. It could be a poster or a book. It could be a brochure or a magazine. I wanted you to look and see how these publications are set up visually so you can then design your own. Tomorrow you will begin thinking about what type of piece you want to create!

Once after teaching this lesson, I overheard a student talking excitedly to another child about the activity. Through the conversation, I got a sense that she understood the lesson deeply, so I asked why she thought we took time to look at how authors set up their publications. This was her reply: "So, because when we do our books, we can kind of copy what they are doing. We could do it a different way or we could do it the same way." Although she struggled to articulate her understanding it was clear to me she made an important connection. She saw how these publications would serve as mentor texts as she and her classmates planned their own pieces. That was the moment I realized this lesson was successful.

Lesson 10: Choosing What Type of Piece to Publish (1-2 Days)

Once students have familiarized themselves with various ways information can be presented, it's time for them to decide what type of nonfiction piece they'll create. This lesson focuses mostly on conferencing with students to help guide them as they decide which type of text would best present the information they have gathered about their topic. Once students have made their decision, they write a letter explaining their choice and why they made it. This is often completed as a homework assignment.

MATERIALS

- Books, magazines, posters, and brochures set up in the same stations as Lesson 9
- Chart created in Lesson 9
- Conferencing notebook

MINI-LESSON

> **Mrs. Gilpin:** We've been working on our animal projects, and so far we've gathered a lot of information. We've taken notes on our animals,

Teaching Students to Conduct Short Research Projects © 2015 by Ryan K. Gilpin, Scholastic Teaching Resources

and now we're moving into the next part of this project: creating a plan for our texts. We spent some time over the past couple of days looking at various types of nonfiction to get an idea of how authors can organize their information. Let's take a quick look at our notes from yesterday.

I quickly review the chart from the previous lesson with students' observations about different types of nonfiction pieces. I do this fairly quickly because my goal for this lesson is to conference with everyone about what kind of text each one is going to choose for his or her project. Sometimes, with a larger class, conferencing can take two days.

Mrs. Gilpin: I want you to take a moment and think about the observations you made over the last two days [or day] and the information you have about your animal. Now think about what types of text would be best for you, or which one seems like you'd have fun creating. Today you will be visiting the stations again, but this time you'll visit only the ones you're most interested in, to decide what to create and to choose a mentor text. A mentor text is a text that will help you as you create your plan. I am going to be conferencing with each of you about what you are interested in, and I'll answer any questions you might have. Once you've made your choice, I want you to write a letter to me explaining why you made that particular choice. Don't worry—you don't have to finish it in class; you can complete it at home tonight, so take your time.

WORK TIME/CONFERENCING

Before beginning conferences, I allow about three to five minutes for students to explore the texts. Each of the following conferences represents a common question or struggle students often have during this part of the project. Many students are fairly certain about what they want to create and don't have a lot of questions. Others are still a bit unsure, and some have trouble narrowing down their choices. When I conference, I try to offer assistance without actually making the choice for them. I often have them go back and look at the types of publications they are interested in and look at our chart. This really helps them to narrow their thinking and to see what would work best for them as writers with the information they've gathered.

In the following conference, a student expresses interest in doing a Q&A book, but is concerned because the books she is looking at don't have many nonfiction features and she wants to include many of them throughout her book.

Mrs. Gilpin: Hi, Sheila. I see that you're looking through the Q&A books.

Sheila: Yeah, I think I'd like to do a question-answer book but I can't decide. I'm not doing one animal, but instead doing marsupials, so I will have lots of animals. It's hard.

Mrs. Gilpin: So you're having a hard time deciding what type of text would be best. Have you narrowed it down to a few ideas?

Sheila:	Yeah. I like the question and answer but I also like the National Geographic books. They have all the cool features. I want those too. I like starting with a question and then answering it.
Mrs. Gilpin:	I want you to take some time to look through some of the Q&A books as well as the National Geographic books. I want you to also look at the chart we made about the different publications. Then I will meet back up with you to see if you've made any progress with your decision.

Conferencing with a student

I give her a few minutes to look through the texts before returning to continue the conference. When I meet back up with her my goal is for her to realize she could take things from each type of book and combine them to create her own format.

Mrs. Gilpin:	Now that you've taken a minute to look through these books and our chart what are you thinking?
Sheila:	I really want to do a question-answer book. I want to write paragraphs. But I also want to include features.
Mrs. Gilpin:	One of the project requirements is to include nonfiction features in your writing.
Sheila:	Could I start with a question, and then have my answer but also put in lots of pictures and features and the cool stuff like these books? [*She holds up National Geographic Everything book.*]
Mrs. Gilpin:	Sheila, I think you're onto something. Why don't you write about in your letter to me and think through how that might work.

The next day as she is working on her plan, I will make sure to touch base with her to see how it's going, so I make note of this plan in my conferencing notebook.

The next conference is with a child who is really interested in doing a magazine, but is concerned he doesn't have enough information for multiple articles like magazines have.

Dan:	I really want to do a magazine about chameleons.
Mrs. Gilpin:	That's great. Tell me more about how you would set this up and what you might include.
Dan:	Well, I want to do a comic and puzzles or games. I just am not sure. I don't have enough for a lot of long articles, and the magazines have long articles.
Mrs. Gilpin:	Let's think about this. Do magazines have one long article or many articles about different topics?
Dan:	They have a lot of articles about different things. That's like our subtopics. Maybe I could do an article for each topic!

Teaching Students to Conduct Short Research Projects © 2015 by Ryan K. Gilpin, Scholastic Teaching Resources

Mrs. Gilpin:	I think you are on the right track. I want you to take some time and think about this idea and I will check back with you before the end of writing time today.

To give him time to think about this and look through the magazines again, I go and conference with two or three more students before coming back to him.

Mrs. Gilpin:	Dan, have you thought about what you could do to create a magazine with the information you have about chameleons?
Dan:	I think I like the idea to do little articles. Like maybe a small article or paragraph about chameleons' adaptations, and then about habitat. Like that.
Mrs. Gilpin:	That's a great idea. You can write about that in your letter to me. Then tomorrow when you're working on your plan, see how it works as you set up your magazine.

The following are typical of conferences where students are certain of what type of text they want to do and are excited about it.

Mrs. Gilpin:	Hi, Simon. Have you decided what type of piece you'd like to make?
Simon:	Yeah, a poster.
Mrs. Gilpin:	What made you decide on a poster?
Simon:	I like doing posters. It's big and gives a lot of space to draw pictures.

———————————————————

Mrs. Gilpin:	Hi, Liza! Have you decided what text you're going to create?
Liza:	A brochure. I like that it folds and each folded part can be one of my topics.

SHARING TIME

For sharing in this lesson, students gather in small groups to share with one another what type of product they have chosen to create. In this discussion they will explain to each other why they chose this particular type of nonfiction and what parts they are most excited about.

Mrs. Gilpin:	Now that everyone has a pretty good idea of what format of text you will be writing, I'd like for you to share your ideas with one another. In small groups, you are going to share what you chose and why, and also what you are most excited about as you begin to work on this piece.

The following is one conversation among children in a small group.

Katy:	I'm going to do a book. I like that you can have lots of features on a page with lots of pictures and writing. I can't wait to write my book and illustrate the pictures.
Emily:	I love the National Geographic books so I want to do one like that. I want it to be set up like what they do. Like the ones with lots of writing broken up and big pictures.

Nick:	I'm going to do a poster. I like how it's all in one place and all together.
Evan:	I'm doing a brochure. I like how they fold. It's kind of cool. And I like reading them when we go on vacation.

I wrap up the lesson by reminding students to write about their choice in a letter to me.

Mrs. Gilpin:	I'm very excited about all the interesting ideas I'm hearing! Remember to write about your choice in a letter to me in your writing journal. If you didn't finish during class, please do it for homework.

MAKING IT YOUR OWN

In my experience, students tend to choose the type of text they want to create based on their writing ability. My stronger students tend to choose magazines and newspapers, while struggling students often create a book. No matter the format, students have certain writing requirements they must meet.

Lesson 11: Creating a Plan (2 Days)

Now that students have finished researching and have selected the type of text they'll publish, it's time for them to create a plan. I like to have students lay out their ideas in storyboard format on a sheet of posterboard. Students can divide the posterboard into sections for each page or part of their text, then sketch and make notes about what will appear on each page, including the text features they want to incorporate.

The plan typically takes students two days to complete. To help guide them as they plan, I create a list of the writing requirements I have for the project based on my school's curriculum and state standards; see below. No matter what type of product students have selected, how they design their text to incorporate these requirements is up to them. They will decide if there is a mentor text they want to use to help as they create their plans. During this time I conference with students, answering questions or helping to guide their thinking. In both days' mini-lessons I model how I create my own plan.

MATERIALS

- Posterboard (1 or 2 sheets per student)
- Mentor texts chosen by students in previous lesson
- Pencils
- Writing Requirements sheet (see sample at right)
- Students' notes taken on their topic
- Conferencing notebook

Writing Requirements for Animal Project

1. Include at least two paragraphs. You can write more if you would like. Your paragraphs should include a topic sentence, 3 to 5 supporting details, and a closing sentence.

   Paragraph Topic: _____

   Paragraph Topic: _____

2. Use 5 to 7 features (more if you would like) of nonfiction. The following is a list to help you choose.

Table of Contents	Diagrams	Headings	Maps	Subheadings	Sidebars
Photographs	Fun Facts	Illustrations	Index	Boldface Words	Captions

3. Include a glossary with at least three words and a definition for each.

   Word: _____

   Word: _____

   Word: _____

The Writing Requirements sheet for our animal project

Teaching Students to Conduct Short Research Projects © 2015 by Ryan K. Gilpin, Scholastic Teaching Resources

Mini-Lesson

Mrs. Gilpin: When we began this project we discussed the various steps you would take to complete it. The first step was to conduct research or gather information about your animal. The first part of the second step was to choose the type of nonfiction piece you're going to create. Today you will begin working on the plan or layout for your piece. To help guide you as you create this plan or layout, I have created a checklist of the project's writing requirements. Let's take a look at these requirements.

I hand out the requirements sheet and have students read it.

Mrs. Gilpin: I know you probably have a lot of questions about these project requirements; and once you have created your plans, we'll have many mini-lessons to make sure you know what to do. Right now we're just focusing on the creation of your plans. For this project you are required to write at least two paragraphs, so as you plan you will chose what you want those paragraphs to be about and where they will go in your piece. You will need to use five to seven features of nonfiction throughout your piece. Lastly, you are required to include a glossary with at least three words. You will not be writing all of these things today. Today you are going to begin creating a plan for what your final product is going to look like. I want you to use this requirement sheet as a guide to help you decide what type of writing will go in each section. To help you understand this process, I am going to model for you how I create my plan for a book about koalas. If you're working on a different type of text, I will meet with you in small groups to talk about those, but much of the process is similar to the planning I will show you now.

At this point, I allow students to get comfortable and put the requirement sheet down so they can focus on the lesson. I think aloud as I write my plan. I do not model creating the whole plan, but I do plan a couple of pages of my book to give students a clear understanding of the task. After I model, I spend time conferencing one-on-one with each student to clarify any misunderstandings and answer questions they have. In this lesson I specifically model how to use the requirement sheet and my notes to create a plan for a book.

Mrs. Gilpin: I have decided I want to create a book, and I have also decided what type of book I want it to be. I really like the books in Bobbie Kalman's Life Cycle series, and I know I want my book to be set up similarly to those books. The first thing I'm going to do is divide my posterboard into squares. Each square is going to represent one page of my book. I'm going to number each square. I'm thinking six pages will be enough to share everything I want, so I'll start by making six boxes. If I see I need more later, I can use another piece of posterboard. Okay, on each page I am going to plan what topic I'm going to focus on, what features I want to use, where the writing will go, and where pictures will go. I am going to start with my cover, which is the first square.

I think I'd like the title to be at the top, so I'm going to draw a rectangle and write the word *title* inside of it. I also know I want my name on the cover, so I will add a box at the bottom and write my name inside. In the middle of my cover I would like a big picture of a koala. I'm going to draw a big box and write "picture of a koala in a tree"—that way I know exactly what type of image I want to create.

After modeling the cover, I move on to the next square on my posterboard. The next square is the first page in my book. As I model for students and create my plan, I refer to the requirement sheet to show students how it can guide them as they create their own plans. I also model how my notes may help guide my plan.

Mrs. Gilpin: Since I'm doing a book, I think it makes sense to have a table of contents—and I see that it is one of the features I can choose from the requirement sheet. I can see that my notes are organized by our subtopics, and I think I'll use those for my table of contents. I would like the first section of my book to be *habitat*, so I'll list that first. I see I have notes about life cycle, and I think it would make sense if *life cycle* comes after *habitat*, so I'll list that next in my table of contents.

I continue to model, creating the table of contents and beginning the pages of my book that will be represented in the next two squares of my plan. I often explain to students that the table of contents doesn't need to be planned first—they can just leave a space for it and fill in the specifics after they've planned the rest of the book.

Mrs. Gilpin: I have a lot of topics listed on my table of contents! I will definitely need another sheet of posterboard for my plan. Now that I have my table of contents, I can move on to the next square on my plan. Because I planned my table of contents, I know that the next square should be about habitat. First I want to look through my notes and see how much information I have. This will help me when I'm deciding how much writing will go on the page and what features I want to use.

I read over my notes out loud and begin to plan the pages about habitat.

Mrs. Gilpin: I can see I have a lot of information about habitat. I think I will write about where in the world koalas are found. I really want to have a heading at the top of the page, so I'm going to draw a square here at the top, to represent the heading. Inside of this square I'm going to write the word "Heading." This is so that when I'm drafting the real page I'll remember that I need to include this heading. It will also come in

> ## Teaching Tip
>
> *Students usually have enough information to complete two pages for each subtopic. As they begin writing, they may realize they need or want to make changes to their plan. I emphasize to students that the plan, like their writing, can always be revised.*

Teaching Students to Conduct Short Research Projects © 2015 by Ryan K. Gilpin, Scholastic Teaching Resources

handy when I'm working on my final copy. On my first page I also want to include a paragraph about Australia and a map. To help me when I'm drafting and publishing, I'll put a box with the words "Paragraph about Australia" to represent where the paragraph will go on this page. I'm going to draw a box and write the word "Map" inside to show that I'll have a map on this page. I think I'll also include a Fun Fact here.

After modeling one more page, I explain what the students will do during their work time. I also explain that I will meet with a small group to discuss how this process works when creating a plan for a poster or brochure.

Mrs. Gilpin:	Today you're going to begin creating your plan. You have the requirement sheet of what you need to include, and you have your notes. These will help guide you through this process. I'm going to meet with small groups to discuss how to create plans for a brochure, magazine, or poster.

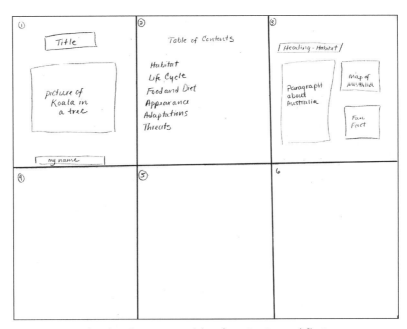

My plan for the cover, table of contents, and first page

WORK TIME/CONFERENCING

I start conferencing by meeting with small groups based on what type of text they are creating. By meeting with these small groups, I can quickly model what it looks like to plan each type of text, and students can begin working on their plans.

When I confer with individual students about their plans, I allow each student to lead the discussion. As they share, I bring up points to focus on and ask questions to help guide their work. I also take notes so that I know which students I need to check in with first the next day.

Mrs. Gilpin:	Emily, tell me about your plan so far.
Emily:	I'm on *appearance*, and I don't really have that many notes, so I

think I might just do one page. I have a fun fact about the smallest squirrel in the world. That kind of fits in, so I want to put a fact box in that section. I'm planning to use real pictures, but I'm not sure what pictures I want.

Mrs. Gilpin: It looks like you're off to a good start. I like how you're using your notes to help guide your plan. How are you feeling about your book now that you've started to put your plan together?

Emily: I'm feeling good about it. I feel like it's going to be a good book.

Mrs. Gilpin: Why do you feel good about it?

Emily: I've been working really hard, and I've been reading a lot and taking notes. I feel like I have a lot of good facts to make a good book.

Students working on their plans

This next conference is with a child who was struggling to organize the pages in a meaningful way. His plan shows diagrams for *appearance* in the *food and diet* section. I don't want to tell him how to organize it but merely want to guide his thinking about the book. When I approach him, he is sketching a food chain diagram.

Mrs. Gilpin: Greg, tell me about your plan.

Greg: I'm working on my *food and diet* section, and I'm going to do a diagram of a food chain.

Mrs. Gilpin: I think that is a great idea for *food and diet*. Let's look at your plan. As I'm looking it over, I see you have a page on appearance, then a page on life cycle, and then three pages on food and diet. Do you have enough information in your notes to do three pages on food and diet?

Greg: Oh! No, I meant two pages and then *adaptations* for two pages!

Mrs. Gilpin: Why don't you go ahead and make that change to your plan and then we'll look at a few of your pages. Here, on this page I see you put another diagram on your *food and diet* page. What is this diagram of?

Teaching Students to Conduct Short Research Projects © 2015 by Ryan K. Gilpin, Scholastic Teaching Resources

| Greg: | A diagram of a snake and the parts of the body. |
| Mrs. Gilpin: | You have it on a page with food and diet. Do you think this is the best section in your book to put this diagram in? |

He pauses and thinks.

| Greg: | Probably not. It's not really what they eat. |
| Mrs. Gilpin: | If you're drawing a diagram to show the parts of a snake's body, which of the topics we researched do you think this diagram would go with best? Let's look at your notes. |

Greg begins looking at his notes and almost immediately sees his mistake.

Greg:	I think it's *appearance*—that's where I wrote down the stuff about their body parts. Yeah, *appearance*. It's showing what a snake looks like.
Mrs. Gilpin:	So you have this diagram of a snake here on page five, but when I look at your plan you have the page with *appearance* at the beginning. As I point that out, what are you thinking?
Greg:	I should have the diagram on this page. [*He points to appearance page.*]
Mrs. Gilpin:	Let's look at the plan for that page. Is there room to add this diagram?
Greg:	Not really. I could add a page about appearance. Can I have two pages about appearance?
Mrs. Gilpin:	Well, is that what you would want to do? Do you have enough information in your notes to support two pages of writing about appearance?
Greg:	I think I can do this one like I have it planned. [*He points to his* appearance *page.*] And then I can have one with just my diagram, just the picture, but like the whole page. But I have this square as *life cycle*. Can I change it?
Mrs. Gilpin:	Remember, Greg, this is your plan. It's much like a draft, so yes, you can change things around as you work with your notes and organize the information the way you want it to be presented in your book.
Greg:	Okay, I think I'll do two *appearance* pages here, and move this one [*he points to the* life cycle *page*] to the page after my diagram of the snake's body.

In these next two conferences, I focus on why the students have selected certain nonfiction text features and how they were thinking about their readers as they planned. Later, I have them share with the class so that everyone can make the connection between what they are planning and the readers who will eventually enjoy and learn from their publications.

| Mrs. Gilpin: | Katy, I can see you're almost finished with your plan. Can you share with me what you've done? |
| Katy: | Well, there are pages, and each one will have at least one paragraph, and each page has at least one picture, and some have headings. |

Mrs. Gilpin:	Let's take a look. On page three you've opted to do a heading. Why?
Katy:	So people will know they're reading about appearance. That's why I have headings—so they know what the page will be about.
Mrs. Gilpin:	I see you have two diagrams in your plan—one for *life cycle* and one for *food and diet*. What made you decide that these two topics would be a good place to include a diagram?
Katy:	Well, for *life cycle* it would be a circle with the different stages of their life.
Mrs. Gilpin:	Why a diagram and not a paragraph?
Katy:	It makes it more exciting to look at if it's not just all writing. And it shows the order.
Mrs. Gilpin:	What about *food and diet*? Why a diagram there?
Katy:	Well, it starts with dolphins, and it goes around to what they eat. The diagram will help readers know what the food chain is.

Katy is very aware of how each of the features she'd selected could best be utilized to help her reader learn new information. Katy has gone from understanding how she, herself, would use these features to thinking about her readers and how they will read her book.

Mrs. Gilpin:	Evan, can you tell me a little about your plan and what you've done for your brochure so far?
Evan:	I have the title, and a picture on the cover, a squid and an octopus. I'd like to compare the two. So on the first page, I have a heading that will probably say "Habitat" or something like that.
Mrs. Gilpin:	Why did you choose a heading here?
Evan:	Because it would prepare the reader for what they're about to be reading, and kind of explain what this is mainly going to be about. When I read books, the headings help me know about the page before I read it, so I want to do that.
Mrs. Gilpin:	What other features do you have in this section of your brochure?
Evan:	I have two maps—a map for squid and a map for octopuses. And then I also have a paragraph and bold words.
Mrs. Gilpin:	Why bold words?
Evan:	Because we are required to make a glossary, and I decided to make those words bold, so readers are likely to think that they'll be in the glossary. They can look them up.
Mrs. Gilpin:	How about this diagram in *food and diet*? What will that be?
Evan:	It's a food chain. I think I can pull it off. It will show how they are connected—like this is connected to that animal, and that animal is connected to another. Like that.

Both students were clearly thinking about how to use these features to better their writing and how they would help their readers make sense of their publications.

Teaching Students to Conduct Short Research Projects © 2015 by Ryan K. Gilpin, Scholastic Teaching Resources

SHARING TIME

After students complete their plans, I allow them the opportunity to share with one another what they have created. This gets them even more excited about the next step: drafting their writing.

Mrs. Gilpin:	Wow! You're all off to a great start with your plans. As we close today, I want you to take a moment to think about why you're creating these texts and whom you're creating them for. As I was conferencing with some of you, I could see you were thinking of your readers as you created the plan. Would anyone like to share what they were thinking about as they worked today?
Evan:	I had a heading on one page to help my readers know what they would read about in that section.
Liza:	And I have a lot of pictures. I want it to be bright.
Hunter:	I have a map so they will know where giraffes live.
Liam:	Me too! I have a map so they'll know where platypuses are.
Mrs. Gilpin:	These are all great examples. It's important to think about your readers as you write. You want to think about what you'd like them to learn and how you can best present the information so they can learn new things about your animals. One way to do that is to think about the features of nonfiction. When we think about what it's like when we read nonfiction, we can remember to use these features as we plan our own writing. We can ask ourselves, "What features would be best used to present this information?" Tomorrow we will continue to work on our plans so that we can begin to draft our writing next week!

A month or so after competing this project, I was having a parent conference with a mother who asked about a social studies project that was due soon. She was concerned that her son had too much work to do because he had to plan his poster and then create it. She felt that it was taking too much time to do both, and she wanted to know why I was requiring students to plan the poster before creating it. I explained to her that students were not required to create a plan for their poster, but I told her about the animal project, and how the children had created plans for their final projects. Apparently her son was using this new skill, even when it wasn't required. This mother went from feeling irritated at all the work her son had to do, to being impressed that he was applying a new skill independently. When learning is meaningful and engaging, students begin applying new skills in other situations, on their own.

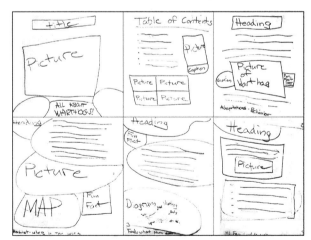

Plan for a book

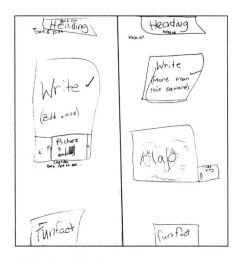 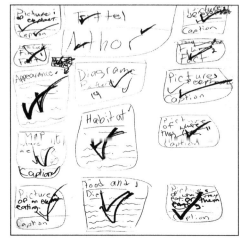

Plan for a brochure   *Plan for a poster*

Assessment for Step Three: Create a Plan for the Product

For this part of the project I assess two things: How students chose their nonfiction text type, and how they developed their plan for creating it. When reviewing their text type choices, I look for how well they explained their reasoning and their understanding of what type of text to use. When looking at their plans, I assess how well they used their notes and the requirement sheet to plan their final product.

Chapter 4

Putting the Plan Into Action

After students have completed their research, taken notes, and developed a plan for their final product, it's time for them to create a draft. In this chapter, the lessons focus on how to get students started with their writing and some key skills they need to help strengthen their writing. I begin this part of the project by conducting a quick review of the writing process we use in my class and then giving them time to write. After students have drafted most of their writing, I conduct lessons on paragraphs and text structure, which help them revise and edit their work. Once they've revised and edited, students are ready to publish their work and share it with others (the subject of Chapter 5). On page 80, I have included a list of other mini-lessons that I often conduct while students are in the process of writing their drafts; select which ones you prefer, based on your students needs.

Chapter 4 Lessons

- Reviewing the Writing Process: Draft, Revise, Edit (1 Day)
- Putting the Plan Into Action (1–3 Days)
- Writing Paragraphs (1–2 Days)
- Text Structures: Description, Compare and Contrast, Sequential (2 Days)
- Text Structures: Cause and Effect, Problem and Solution (3 Days)

Lesson 12: Reviewing the Writing Process: Draft, Revise, Edit (1 Day)

This lesson consists only of a mini-lesson because it's simply a review of the writing process we've already been working on in my classroom. From the first day of school, students are introduced to and follow the same process: prewrite, draft, revise, edit, and publish. At this point in our research project, I do a quick review of these steps and the anchor charts we have hanging up as references. After students have had time to draft, I review the process again to focus them on revision and editing. I also provide a checklist that students can use as a guide as they move through the writing process. You can use the checklist provided on page 124, or create your own based on your teaching style and the skills you want your students to focus on.

MATERIALS

- Chart paper and markers
- Writing Process anchor charts
- Research Project Writing-Process Checklist (page 124)
- Conferencing notebook

Mini-Lesson

Mrs. Gilpin:	Today before you begin writing I want to do a quick review of the writing process with you. I'd like for everyone to look at the anchor charts we have hanging on the wall. Let's look at the first step of the writing process.
Emily:	We have to prewrite.
Liza:	I like to make lists when I prewrite.
Noah:	I like to use webs to connect ideas.
Mrs. Gilpin:	Yes, making lists and drawing webs are two ways we prewrite. What kinds of prewriting have you done for your research project?
Evelyn:	We have notes on what we read.
Liam:	And we made our plans!
Mrs. Gilpin:	Yes. So you have already done some prewriting. You took notes, you created a plan for your final products, and now you are ready for the next step! What is that next step in the writing process?
Noah:	Draft.
Mrs. Gilpin:	What do we do when we are drafting?
Fin:	We just write. We need to get our ideas and writing down.

Mrs. Gilpin:	Exactly. When drafting, you want to take your notes and your plan and just write. Remember, when you are writing your draft, you don't need to worry about spelling. If you know you have trouble with a particular word, you can circle it so when you go back to check your spelling you'll know to check that word. What is the next step we have to follow when writing?
Shelia:	Revising and seeing if it makes sense.
Mrs. Gilpin:	Great. Once we have completed our draft we then go back and read through it. We ask ourselves, "Does what I wrote make sense?" We are looking at how it is organized, whether we have complete sentences, and whether we need to add details. Over the next few days I'm going to do some lessons that will help you revise your work. What do we do once we've revised our work?
Doug:	We edit. Check spelling and capitals.
Lisa:	We also look at punctuation. Like periods or question marks.
Mrs. Gilpin:	Yes, we then check spelling, punctuation, and capital letters. After we have checked to see if our writing is organized and makes sense, then we look at the mechanics. Once we've checked our drafts for all these things, we move onto publishing. This is when we write a final copy of our draft with all of the changes we made to it. As you're working on the writing for this project, don't forget to reference this chart. It will help you to complete all of the things you need to do before you can publish. To help with this I have created a checklist for you to keep as you're working. As we work on our writing over the next few days, I want you to make sure you have done each thing on this list, including having friends read your work and give feedback.

The Writing Process

1. Prewrite - Pick the topic. Plan the Writing. Graphic Organizer.

2 Draft - Jist Write! Write the Story. Dont worry about Spelling, Capitals, and Punctuation! Don't Erase!

3. Revise - 1. Read your Writing. 2. Ask "Does it make Sense?" Add details or take out details. 3 Read your writing again.

4. Edit - Check Spelling. Check Punctuation. Check Capital letters

5. Publish - Write the final Copy on fresh paper. Include the changes you made. Use your best cursive. Type it.
- Make a cover
- Illustrations

Anchor charts summarizing the writing process

Peer Editing

At the beginning of the year after students have been introduced to the writing process and have completed at least one writing piece, I introduce peer editing. The most important part of peer editing is helping students understand the importance of keeping their feedback positive while at the same time helping make each other's writing better. I spend about a week modeling this for students using their writing as examples. Below is a checklist I created to help them edit one another's work:

* Keep your feedback positive!

* Read your friends work two times and ask, "Does this make sense?"

* If there is something that doesn't make sense, ask your partner to explain or retell that part of the writing.

* Share with your friend two or three things you really liked about the writing.

* Offer to help your partner with spelling.

* Ask your partner if they need help with anything else and work together on those things.

Lesson 13: Putting the Plan Into Action (1–3 Days)

For this lesson, I model how to put notes and a plan together to create a draft. After modeling, I conference with students about their own writing. I usually take two days to model this drafting process when students are beginning to write; you can adjust the time you spend based on your students' needs. I like to leave plenty of time for my students to write without worrying about revising and editing just yet. Usually with the help of their notes and plan, drafting comes fairly easily to students.

MATERIALS

* Students' notes
* Students' plans
* Chart paper and markers
* Conferencing notebook

Mini-Lesson

Mrs. Gilpin: Today is a really big day on this project. You will begin writing the draft for your nonfiction piece! To do this, you will need your notes, your plan, and draft paper just like I have here.

As I talk, I model writing my own draft.

Mrs. Gilpin: The first thing I do is gather together my notes and the plan I created for my book about koalas. Today I am going to start with my *habitat* section. I can see in my plan I have a heading, a paragraph, a map, and a fun fact laid out. I am going to get my draft paper and write what page of my book this is a draft of. Since it's page three of my plan, I'll write that at the top of my draft paper. This is so that when I begin to publish my book I will know what page this is a draft of. As I look at my plan, I can see that I have a heading and I need to draft that. I know headings are like a title and get my readers ready for what they are going to read about, so I think I will call this section "Koala's Paradise." I am going to write the word "Heading" on my draft paper and next to it I will write my title, "Koala's Paradise."

I've planned a paragraph to go under my heading; I'm going to write that tomorrow when we focus specifically on paragraphs, so I'll just leave space for it now.

I move on to the next two features on the page, which are a map and a fun fact. Again, as I talk to the students I model the writing.

Mrs. Gilpin: Next I'm going to move on to my map. As I look through my notes I see that koalas are found in the eastern states of Australia. In my book I would like to have a map of Australia and then color in the parts of Australia where koalas can be found. I'm going to sketch it quickly on my draft, and I'll draw and color the map when I publish. I also see that I have a fun fact planned for this page. I am going to write "Fun Fact" on my draft paper and then look through my notes to see if I have a fact I would like to use for my habitat section.

I read aloud through a few of my notes.

Mrs. Gilpin: I think this is a great fact to use, so I'm going use it as my fun fact: "Scientists have found fossils of koalas from 20 million years ago!"

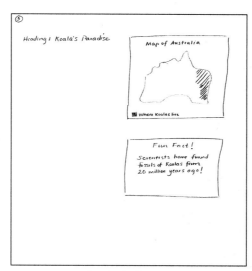

Draft of a habitat page

I let students know this is just one way they can draft their features. I also explain that they can draft the page or section as it will look with the writing in the correct places.

Mrs. Gilpin: Now I'm ready to draft the next section of my book, *life cycles*. On a new sheet of draft paper I will write "page 4" so I know what section of my book this draft is for. Now I will draft each piece of writing I have on my plan. This time I'm going to model it a little differently. Instead of writing the feature on my draft paper and then drafting the actual writing, I'm going to actually draft the page of my book, as it will look when I publish.

I again model drafting a page of my book based on what I have on the plan.

Mrs. Gilpin: This section focuses on my animal's life cycle. Again, I'm going to draft one feature at a time. First, I'll draft my heading. Since it is at the top of the page in my plan, I'll write it at the top of my draft paper. I'm focusing on koala mothers and babies and I'll call this section "A Mother's Love."

On the top of my draft paper I write A Mother's Love.

Mrs. Gilpin: I also see that I have a diagram of the life cycle in the center of the page on my plan. I know I need to sketch a draft of that. For my sketch, I'll include an embryo, a baby, and an adult. I am not going to draw the actual pictures because that might take me a long time, but I'm going to label the diagram so I know when I publish what I want the illustrations to be.

I sketch my diagram in the center of my draft paper.

Mrs. Gilpin: Next I see I had planned to write three bulleted facts at the bottom of my page. Again I am going to look through my notes for information about mother koalas and their babies.

I continue to draft this page while thinking aloud for students to observe, focusing on taking a note and turning the fragments in my notes into complete sentences.

Mrs. Gilpin: I see here my notes say "stay with mom for 10–12 months." I'm ready to draft my first bullet, but the note I have is not a complete sentence. For my sentence to be complete, I need a subject and the information I'm giving about my subject. I'm going to write as one of my bullets, "A koala baby stays with its mother for about a year before going off on its own."

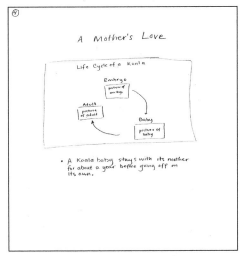

Draft of a life cycles page

Teaching Students to Conduct Short Research Projects © 2015 by Ryan K. Gilpin, Scholastic Teaching Resources

After I finish these two pages, I explain to students what they'll be doing during their work time.

Mrs. Gilpin: Today you will begin drafting the various pieces of writing and features you've laid out in your plan. I showed you two ways that you can draft your publication: you can write the name of the feature and then draft that particular piece of writing, or you can draft the page, exactly as it will look in your book or in the section of your brochure or poster. I will be coming around to conference with you as you start your drafts. Remember, drafts are where you "just write." We will revise and edit our work later.

WORK TIME/CONFERENCING

Although students use their notes to help create their plan, they often run into problems as they begin to write. I encourage students to make whatever changes to their plans they see fit, as long as they can explain their reasoning for these changes. Often students think that once their plan is done it's set in stone. This is a great opportunity for them to learn how writing can be revised and edited many times before it's actually complete. My first conference is with a student who realized once he began writing his draft that what he has in his plan doesn't work.

Evan: I realized I didn't have enough notes on appearance. I can't do a full paragraph, captions, and fun facts like I have on this page.

Mrs. Gilpin: What are you thinking about doing?

Evan: I think I should change my plan, but I don't know if I can. Can I change it now, or do I have to do it like I have here?

Mrs. Gilpin: It sounds like you don't have enough information to make what you have in your plan work, so I think revising your plan might make sense. What are you thinking about doing instead?

Evan: I was thinking about features and the list you gave us, and I decided to transfer the information to something else.

Mrs. Gilpin: What are you thinking of doing instead?

Evan: I decided to transfer the information I was going to use in the paragraph into two separate diagrams. A diagram for the body of the octopus and a diagram for the body of the squid.

Mrs. Gilpin: Why do you think that is a better option for your brochure?

Evan: Well, because diagrams only require you to know what the animal or plant has on it and where it is. And then you just put that on paper in a picture and label it. They can really show what the squid and octopus look like instead of me writing it in sentences.

Mrs. Gilpin: I think this might work for you. What would you include in your diagram?

Evan: I'm thinking I can label the different body parts and when I'm done, I can have a sentence or bullets about their size and how big they are or something like that.

| Mrs. Gilpin: | I think you're ready to revise your plan with your new ideas, and then you can start to draft this page. At the end of our writing workshop I'd like you to share with the class what you worked on today. I think this could really help your classmates who run into the same problem as they're working. |

My second conference is with a student who realized he has more information in his notes than he's included in his plan. He took excellent notes but as he started to draft he realized his plan didn't contain all the information he had gathered. He's unsure if he should revise his plan or leave out some information.

Liam:	I am working on my *habitat* page and I don't know how I can fit all of my notes here.
Mrs. Gilpin:	Let's take a look at your plan to see what you were going to do on this page.
Liam:	I want to do a picture with a caption, two fun facts, and a paragraph.
Mrs. Gilpin:	Let's take a look at your notes.

He starts to look at his notes.

Liam:	I'm not sure how to fit it all. I have all of this information about their burrows and the riverbanks, but I have a lot about Australia, too.
Mrs. Gilpin:	Why are you thinking this might not fit?
Liam:	I think I should do two pages. One page about Australia, and one about the river and burrow and the platypuses' home. Can I change my plan?
Mrs. Gilpin:	I don't see why you can't make some changes to your plan, and I think adding an additional page about habitat is a great idea. Why don't you go ahead and work on revising your plan, and then you can begin drafting these two pages about habitat.

SHARING TIME

| Mrs. Gilpin: | Let's take a moment and think about the work you did today drafting your piece. What was easy? What was challenging? Share at your tables how it went for you, and then we'll discuss these successes and challenges together. |

After a few moments, I begin the discussion.

Mrs. Gilpin:	Let's start with what went well for you today.
Katy:	It was really easy to do my table of contents because I already had my plan and each page was labeled; so I knew what information to put in my table of contents and how to do it.
Beth:	Yeah, mine too, because I already knew that *habitat* was first, so I knew that it would be page one in my table of contents.

Mrs. Gilpin:	Having a plan can really help when you get started because you have already thought about where your information will go. You've already organized your writing in some way by creating a plan! What else went well today?
Greg:	Sometimes drafts are hard because I never know what to write. Having my notes and my plan helped me get started right away today. I knew what to do!
Hunter:	I knew to draft my *habitat* page with a heading because of my plan, and my notes gave me an idea of what to call that page.
Mrs. Gilpin:	I am hearing again that having your notes and your plan made drafting easier. Did anyone experience a challenge today while drafting?
Evan:	I realized when I got started on my draft of the pages about appearance that I didn't have enough information to write a paragraph. A paragraph didn't seem like a good idea, so I transferred my information to a diagram of a squid and labeled it.
Liam:	I had to work on my plan too. I had a ton of information about habitat but my plan only had room for a little bit, so I added a page and now it fits. I think it's really good.
Liza:	You can change your plan?
Evan:	Mrs. Gilpin said we could revise them and make changes if it works.
Mrs. Gilpin:	Yes! As you begin drafting, you may find that your plan doesn't quite fit with the information you have, even though you used your notes to plan it! Revising your plan and draft numerous times might be necessary. When your favorite authors write books, they revise and edit many, many times before their book is published. You all are learning what it is like to be an author!
Fin:	Wow! That's cool!
Doug:	I get to be an author?
Mrs. Gilpin:	We are all authors!

MAKING IT YOUR OWN

The topics in the box on page 80 are just examples of the lessons I often conduct with students as they're writing their drafts. As your students begin to write, you will see what types of issues they're struggling with or need to review. These can be turned into mini-lessons as well. The most important thing about the mini-lessons you teach while students are actively writing is that they support what the students are doing or need the most practice with to become better writers.

Teaching Tip

There is real magic when kids realize they are authors. I encourage you to call your students authors at every opportunity. It boosts their confidence, gives them a real sense of accomplishment, and allows them to take great pride in their work.

Mini-Lesson Topics

These are some of the mini-lessons I commonly teach during this portion of the research project, to the whole class, small groups, or in conferences, depending on how many students need the lesson. This is just a sampling—choose the lessons your students show you they need.

* Getting started with drafting

* Turning notes into complete sentences

* Writing complete sentences (versus sentence fragments and run-ons)

* Combining ideas into more complex sentences

* Creating specific text features, such as bullets, captions, headings

* Creating graphics, such as a diagram, chart, or map

* Using commas in a series

* Reviewing correct punctuation and capitalization

* Using homonyms correctly, such as *there*, *their*, and *they're*

* Forming plurals correctly

Lesson 14: Writing Paragraphs (1-2 Days)

One of the writing skills I spend a lot of time on when doing any research project is paragraph writing, which helps students learn how to organize their writing in meaningful ways and gives them opportunities to practice various writing styles. I start paragraph writing early in the year, but when we do research projects I dig a little deeper into this type of writing. Before conducting this lesson, I have completed lessons on the parts of a paragraph: topic sentence, body, and closing sentence. The first half of the lesson reviews the parts of a paragraph, while the second focuses on modeled writing. You can do the lesson in one or two days, depending on your students.

MATERIALS

* Chart paper and markers
* Paragraph graphic organizer (page 125)
* Notes for modeling
* Publication plan for modeling
* Conferencing notebook

Teaching Students to Conduct Short Research Projects © 2015 by Ryan K. Gilpin, Scholastic Teaching Resources

Day One: The Parts of a Paragraph

Mini-Lesson

My students have had previous experiences with paragraph writing, but this lesson can be adapted as an introductory lesson to paragraph writing if your students are new to it.

Mrs. Gilpin: As you were working on your plans you may have noticed one of the requirements was to have at least two paragraphs in your publication. Over the next few days we'll be learning more about how to write paragraphs. First of all, let's think about what a paragraph *is*. Take a moment to gather your thoughts and then turn to the person next to you to share.

Once students have had a chance to turn and talk, I begin the discussion. As we discuss, I create an anchor chart for students to use as reference.

Mrs. Gilpin: What do you think of when we are talking about paragraph writing?

Noah: Sentences.

Evan: A topic.

Mrs. Gilpin: Yes! A paragraph is a group of sentences working together to give information or focus on one particular topic. There are three parts to a paragraph: the topic sentence, the body, and the closing sentence. Today we will review each part and create a chart to help when you are writing. When writing a paragraph it's important to introduce your reader to your topic. We do this by starting paragraphs with a topic sentence. This gets your readers ready for the specific information they're about to read. Once you have introduced your topic, you're ready to move on to the next part. Does anyone know what that is?

Mary: You write the body, the details, the information.

Mrs. Gilpin: Yes! The next part of a paragraph is the body. That's where you will write the details you want to share. Usually you will have three to five details about your topic to put in your paragraph. Let's look at the next and final part, the closing sentence.

Simon: Is that the end sentence? That's hard.

Mrs. Gilpin: The closing sentence comes at the end of your paragraph and reminds your reader of the topic you first introduced. This is tricky because you don't want to repeat your topic sentence, but you want to remind the reader of your overall focus. Keep these ideas in mind as you continue drafting today.

> Parts of Paragraph
> Most paragraphs have three parts.
>
> 1. Topic Sentence - Introduces the main idea.
>
> 2. The Body - Explains or describes the main idea. Details (3-5)
>
> 3. Closing Sentence - Reminds the reader what the paragraph was about.
>
> 5 - 7 Sentences

Anchor chart on parts of a paragraph

This is only meant to be a quick review; as I model my writing in the next half of the lesson and conference with students, I will go into more depth about these three parts.

This next part of the lesson can be done in one or two days, depending on the needs of your students.

Mrs. Gilpin: I am going to share with you how to use a graphic organizer to help plan a paragraph, and then I will model how to use that organizer to help write the paragraph.

Review the chart with students as needed.

Mrs. Gilpin: Now I am ready to begin working on my graphic organizer to plan my paragraph.

There are many great organizers available to help students with paragraph writing. On page 125, I've included one I used with this project, but feel free to use another if you have a particular favorite.

Modeled Writing: Using the Paragraph Graphic Organizer

I model how I use the organizer to plan my paragraph.

Getting Started

Mrs. Gilpin: To start, I need my graphic organizer, my notes, and my plan. I see that my notes aren't in any particular order, and I need to think of a way to organize them as I write. I don't want to just turn my notes into sentences and put them together, because then my paragraph might not be as organized as it could be. I need to put this information together in a meaningful way. To help with this, I will use a paragraph graphic organizer. I can see in my notes that I have the phrases "eucalyptus forest," "warm climate," and "Australia." I see "New South Wales, Victoria, and Queensland." I also see that it says "southern hemisphere."

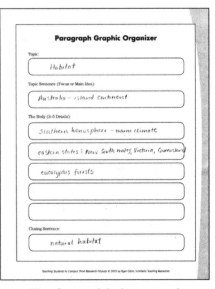

Plan for modeled paragraph

Choosing an Idea for the Topic Sentence

Mrs. Gilpin: The first part of the organizer asks for the topic. My focus is habitat, so I will write that in the section that says "Topic." Then the organizer says "Topic Sentence." When I look at my notes they are all about Australia, so I want that to be my paragraph's main idea. I know from my research that Australia is an island continent, and that is important. For my topic sentence I will write "Australia" and "island continent." I think when I begin writing, I'll open my

Teaching Students to Conduct Short Research Projects © 2015 by Ryan K. Gilpin, Scholastic Teaching Resources

paragraph with a sentence stating that koalas live in Australia, since this will help my reader understand that my paragraph will only be about Australia.

Listing the Details

Mrs. Gilpin: Now I'm ready to get to the details. On my organizer, I'm just going to list them, not write the sentences. My details are *southern hemisphere*, *warm climate*, *eastern states*, *New South Wales*, *Victoria*, *Queensland*, and *eucalyptus forests*. When I write my paragraph, I'll use this list to write sentences that will make up the body of my paragraph. That is where I'm sharing the specific information I want my reader to learn about where in Australia koalas live.

Choosing an Idea for the Closing Sentence

Mrs. Gilpin: The closing sentence is always hardest for me! I know I don't want to repeat my topic sentence, but I do want to bring my readers back to the main idea that koalas live in Australia. On my graphic organizer I'm going to write "natural habitat," since Australia is the only place koalas can be found in the wild. That will remind my reader of my topic! Now I'm ready to begin writing my paragraph using complete sentences. Looking at my organizer and the key words or phrases I have listed will help me to organize my information.

Modeled Writing: Paragraph

Now I model how to use the organizer to write a paragraph.

Writing the Topic Sentence

Mrs. Gilpin: Looking at my graphic organizer I see the words *Australia* and *island continent*. I want the topic sentence to introduce my reader to what the paragraph will be about. I know from my research that koalas live in Australia, so I will open my paragraph with this sentence: "Koalas live on the island continent of Australia." This lets my reader know they will be reading about koalas living in Australia.

Writing the Body or Details

Mrs. Gilpin: Now I'm ready to give the reader details about where in Australia koalas can be found, and what it's like there. I see on my organizer that I have quite a few things listed. I think I should start by giving a little more information about Australia. My list says "southern hemisphere" and "warm climate." I know that places in the southern hemisphere can have a warm climate, so I will make my sentence about that. My next sentence will be "Australia is in the southern hemisphere and has a very warm climate." Looking at the list on my organizer I see information about where in Australia koalas can be found. I know they live in eucalyptus forests and that Victoria, New South Wales, and Queensland are states found on the eastern side of Australia. I think I'll combine those ideas into one sentence: "Koalas make their homes in the eucalyptus forests in the eastern states of Victoria, New South Wales, and Queensland.

Modeled paragraph

Writing the Closing Sentence

Mrs. Gilpin: Now I'm ready to move on to the closing sentence. I want to remind my reader that my topic was focused on koalas and Australia, but I also want to make sure I'm not repeating my topic sentence and am still providing new information. From my research, I know that Australia is the only place where koalas can be found in their natural habitat. I will focus on that fact and will write, "A koala's natural habitat is found only in Australia, so that's the only place you can see them in the wild!"

After I complete this modeling process, I explain to my students that they will now begin working on their paragraphs.

WORK TIME/CONFERENCING

As they begin working, I conference with each of them about their graphic organizers. The following two conferences are with students who consistently struggled with organizing their writing, and I was fairly certain paragraph writing would be a challenge for them. After conferencing with each, they wrote paragraphs that amounted to some of the best writing they had done all year. Whenever I see this kind of success from students after conferencing, I often copy their work for their portfolio and write at the top "The power of conferencing." It never ceases to amaze me how one five-minute conference can make such a big difference in what my students are able to accomplish.

My first conference is with a student who was really struggling to get started with his graphic organizer. His only goal for the week is to finish his paragraphs. I decide to conference with him first so he can get started with his writing and accomplish that goal.

Mrs. Gilpin: Hi, Greg. Can you show me what you've worked on so far today?

Greg: I have my organizer and I have it for *adaptations*. I have my notes, but I'm confused.

Mrs. Gilpin: Can you explain to me what you're confused about?

Greg: I know that adaptations help my snake to survive, but I'm not sure what to write about.

Mrs. Gilpin: Let's start by looking at the organizer. You said your topic is *adaptations*. Let's go ahead and fill in the first part with that information.

In the section titled Topic he writes "adaptations."

Mrs. Gilpin: You also said that you know they help a snake to survive. Is that going to be your overall focus of the paragraph?

Greg: Yes, I want to tell how they have venom that kills and how snakes can blend in.

Mrs. Gilpin: Why don't you fill in the part of the organizer for your topic sentence with that information?

On the section titled Topic Sentence he writes, "Adaptations help them survive."

Mrs. Gilpin: Great! Now let's move on to the next part of the organizer. Remember that this is where you will write your details or information about adaptations helping a snake to survive. Let's take a moment and think about what we learned in science about adaptations. We can also reference the charts with our subtopics to help.

I want him to recall information he's learned in science, knowing that this information will help him to write his paragraph. After looking at the charts on the wall and thinking for a few moments, he responds.

Greg: There are two adaptations. One is physical, and one is behavior.

Mrs. Gilpin: What does it mean if an adaptation is physical, or behavioral?

Greg: I think physical is when they have something on their body, like the venom, or scales. I think behavior is when they do something, like squeeze their prey.

Mrs. Gilpin: Yes! You have some great information about snakes and their adaptations. Let's look through your notes to make sure you haven't left anything out that you may want to include in your details. Then you can start to list the adaptations you just shared with me.

After looking through his notes, he begins listing his details. On his organizer he writes, "colors help blend in, snakes use venom to kill the prey, snakes squeeze their prey, snakes use scutes to help them move."

Mrs. Gilpin: Greg, I think you have a great list of details here, and your readers will learn a lot of information about snakes and the adaptations they have. Now let's look at your closing sentence. I want you to work on that. In a few minutes I'll check back with you.

Now that he's been successful with two of the sections, I want him to try the final section of the organizer on his own. When I come back, he's moved on to writing his paragraph.

Mrs. Gilpin: I see you have moved on to writing your paragraph! Do you have any questions for me about your closing sentence? I know that can be a bit tricky!

Greg: No, I think it's okay. I think I can write this now.

Mrs. Gilpin:	That's great, Greg. When you're done I'd love to read it and see what you decide for the closing sentence.

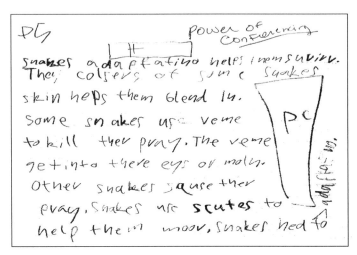

Greg's adaptation *paragraph*

When he finishes he brings me his draft to read. I am very impressed with what he's done. It is clear to the reader what information he is presenting, and it is well organized. Although his closing sentence is a bit weak, he is very proud of the work he's done and so am I. The organizer and our conference really helped him to put his thoughts together so his reader can learn new information about snakes.

My next conference is with a student who has already completed her organizer and written her paragraph. She has some good details about her animal and what it eats, but no clear topic sentence. I decide to start by revising her organizer.

Mrs. Gilpin:	Hi, Evelyn. I see you're busy working on your *food and diet* paragraph. Let's read it together.

Together we read her paragraph. She's written, "Moose love water lilies. Moose eat grass and leaves. In winter moose eat bark because there is nothing to eat. Moose love plants."

Evelyn's first paragraph

After reading her paragraph, I ask to see her organizer. The topic sentence section is blank.

Mrs. Gilpin:	On the organizer you didn't fill out the section for your topic sentence. Why is that?
Evelyn:	I don't know. I think I forgot. No, it was hard, and I didn't know how to do it.
Mrs. Gilpin:	Let's go look at the anchor chart about parts of a paragraph so we can review what a topic sentence is. Go ahead and read it, and then we will discuss it.
Evelyn:	It says it tells the reader what they will learn about. It introduces my topic.
Mrs. Gilpin:	That's right; it gets your reader ready and introduces the topic. Let's take a look at your details. I see you have a lot of information here. What specific information are you sharing about moose?

Evelyn:	They like water lilies, and they eat grass and leaves. In the winter they eat bark. They really like plants. They don't eat meat.
Mrs. Gilpin:	I want you to think about something we learned in science and take a look at the chart we made when we decided what topics to research. What type of eater is a moose? Do they only eat plants? Do they eat plants and animals? Do moose only eat meat?

She looks at the chart and at our science center posters.

Evelyn:	Moose only eat plants. Isn't that an herbivore? Or is that omnivore? No, it's herbivore.
Mrs. Gilpin:	Yes, plant eaters are called herbivores. How could we use this information in your paragraph and include a topic sentence?
Evelyn:	[*thinks for a moment*] I could use that as my topic. Yeah, the topic sentence should be that they are herbivores.
Mrs. Gilpin:	I think that would be a great topic sentence since you're about to give your reader a lot of information about the plants moose eat. Let's fill in that part of the graphic organizer so you can revise your paragraph. There is something else I notice about your paragraph. You wrote that in winter moose eat bark because there is nothing for them to eat. What do they eat in summer?
Evelyn:	In the summer they eat water lilies, grass, and leaves, but in winter it snows. They can't eat the grass if there is snow, but in summer they eat a lot of grass. There isn't much for them in winter. Should I add that or write that? Maybe I should.
Mrs. Gilpin:	That is a great detail that you could add to your writing to help your reader understand why moose eat different things during different seasons. I'm going to write "summer" next to your sentence about water lilies and "add about snow" next to the sentence about bark. Adding those details will give your reader a bit more information. Go ahead and revise your paragraph, and I'll check back with you tomorrow to see what changes you've made.

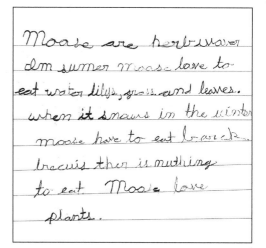

Evelyn's revised paragraph

The next day when I check on Evelyn's writing, she has completed a new paragraph with the topic sentence and details we discussed. It now reads, "Moose are herbivores. In summer moose love to eat water lilies, grass, and leaves. When it snows in winter moose have to eat bark because there is nothing to eat. Moose love plants." Evelyn is so proud of her new paragraph, as am I. For a student who once consistently struggled to put information together in an organized way, this paragraph is a major accomplishment.

SHARING TIME

I have students gather in small groups or with a partner to share a paragraph each wrote. I ask them to share their topic sentences and their closing sentences. Then they swap for peer editing.

Lesson 15: Text Structures: Description, Compare and Contrast, Sequential (2 Days)

For this lesson, I introduce three of the five forms of text structures that authors use when writing nonfiction pieces: description, compare and contrast, and sequential. Although my mini-lesson offers only a brief introduction to each one, during conferences I go into more depth with students. Since students' topics vary, so does their writing and their use of text structures. At times, I will work with small groups of students who are using the same structure to give further instruction or support.

This introductory lesson can be done in a variety of ways. I have completed it in one day, in two days, or I've focused on different text structures, one at a time, over a week. Typically I do this lesson over a two-day period because I'm covering this topic concurrently in my reading workshop while my students are writing. I focus on description, compare and contrast text, and sequential structures in this lesson, and I address cause and effect and problem and solution in Lesson 16. There are many visual resources available for teachers to use when teaching text structures. With my students I create a reference chart, but I also have excellent mini-posters from an article I read on Scholastic Teacher Blogs by Beth Newingham (http://www.scholastic.com/teachers/top_teaching/2011/03/my-march-top-ten-list-nonfiction-reading-resources).

MATERIALS

- Chart paper and markers
- Paragraphs written by students
- Conferencing notebook

Mini-Lesson

Mrs. Gilpin: Today we're going to work on revising the paragraphs we wrote for our projects. Let's take a moment to think about revising. Turn to your neighbor and share one thing you do when revising your work.

I give students a moment to share with each other, then call on a few to share with the whole group.

Mrs. Gilpin: Revising means we might add information, take information out, or rearrange the order of our information to make it clearer and easier for our readers to understand. When writing nonfiction, authors use key words or phrases to show readers how ideas and information are connected. There are five different text structures authors use in nonfiction text. Today we will review three of those text structures. Together we will create a chart with some of the key phrases to help you as you revise your paragraphs. The first structure of nonfiction that authors use is called *description.*

On my chart titled "Text Structure" I write "Description."

Mrs. Gilpin: What do you think it means if an author is using this structure?

Luke: Does it mean they are describing something?

Dan: Yeah, like telling us what something looks like?

Mrs. Gilpin: When authors use this structure they are describing something so that readers can really visualize or see what they are describing. In description, authors use specific and vivid adjectives and verbs to describe people, places, or things and how they might be doing something. For example, instead of saying, "A koala is pretty," I might write, "A koala is a furry animal with gray hair." Or instead of "A jaguar hunts its prey," I might write, "A jaguar likes to climb trees, wait silently, then pounce on its prey from above."

As I'm explaining the structure of description, I'm also filling in the anchor chart that students will use as a reference. The anchor chart lists key words or phrases along with my examples.

Mrs. Gilpin: The next text structure that nonfiction authors often use is called *compare and contrast.*

Mary: Like to compare things?

Lisa: Showing how they are the same?

Noah: What if it's different?

Mrs. Gilpin:	When authors use the structure compare and contrast, they are showing how two or more things are alike or different. Some of the key words or phrases they use to show this structure are: *similar to, alike, different from, same as, on the other hand, although, however, like, unlike, opposites, as opposed to,* and *both*. For example if I want to compare the koala to a kangaroo I might write, "A koala is similar to a kangaroo. Both are marsupials, meaning they have pouches to carry their young." Here I have used the phrase *similar to* and the word *both*. My readers will now understand that I am showing how a kangaroo and koala are alike.
	The third type of text structure that authors use is called *sequential*. That's a big word. What do you think that word might mean?

I give students an opportunity to think and then begin sharing.

Simon:	How something is done?
Shelia:	Order. The order of something.
Mrs. Gilpin:	Yes, sequential is the order in which something happened or happens. Some of the key words authors use to show this structure are: *first, next, second, before, after, last,* and *finally*. These words help a reader to understand the order in which something has been done, needs to be done, or happens. For example, if I'm explaining how to make a sandwich, instead of writing, "You put peanut butter and jelly on the bread and put the bread together," I might write, "First, you get two slices of bread. Then, you put peanut butter on one slice and jelly on the other slice. Next, you put the two slices together and cut the sandwich in half. Finally, you get to share your sandwich with a friend!"

After reviewing these three structures, I explain to the class what they will be doing while writing.

Anchor charts for text structure

Teaching Students to Conduct Short Research Projects © 2015 by Ryan K. Gilpin, Scholastic Teaching Resources

| Mrs. Gilpin: | Today I would like you to take a look at your paragraphs and think about what structure you may already be using, or could use. Then I want you to think how you can revise your text using some of the key words or phrases from the chart and posters. |

WORK TIME/CONFERENCING

Both conferences below are with students who had completed a paragraph and are busy revising when I approach them. They have some good ideas for how to incorporate some of the key words and phrases into their writing to show which structure they are using.

Mrs. Gilpin:	Hi, Lea. Tell me a little about what you're working on.
Lea:	I wrote a paragraph about beavers yesterday, about them building dams, their homes. I am reading it and thinking the structure is the one with the order. It's how they build it.
Mrs. Gilpin:	Do you mean sequential?
Lea:	Yes! I think that is the one I have in my paragraph because I am writing how they make their dams. I looked at the words, and I think I can use *first*.
Mrs. Gilpin:	Show me where you are thinking about using the word *first*. Read the sentence you wrote yesterday. Then read it to me with the change you think you will make.
Lea:	Here it says, "Beavers chop down trees in order to make their homes." I think I will change it to, "First, beavers chop down trees in order to make their homes."
Mrs. Gilpin:	Is that the first step they take to make a home?
Lea:	Yes, they need to chop the wood first.
Mrs. Gilpin:	Using the word *first* will help your reader understand that it is the first step. What other changes were you thinking of making to this paragraph?
Lea:	The next sentence says, "Beavers use mud hard as iron to protect the dam." I think I am going to use the word *then*.

Lea writes the word then *at the start of that sentence so it reads, "Then, beavers use mud hard as iron to protect the dam."*

| Mrs. Gilpin: | Lea, take a moment to think about your readers. How will these changes help them as they read your work? |
| Lea: | Maybe they will know how beavers make their dams. Maybe they will know what happens first. |

My next conference is with another student who is working on revising a paragraph.

| Mrs. Gilpin: | Hi, Evan. Tell me about your paragraph. |
| Evan: | Well, I'm working on my paragraph comparing squids and octopuses and their habitats. |

Mrs. Gilpin:	Please explain what text structure this paragraph is following.
Evan:	I am looking at compare and contrast. I am explaining how squids and octopuses live in the ocean but can be found in different parts and sometimes the same parts. I am making some changes using words from the chart.
Mrs. Gilpin:	What changes are you making? Can you read a sentence you wrote and then read it with the change you are thinking of making?

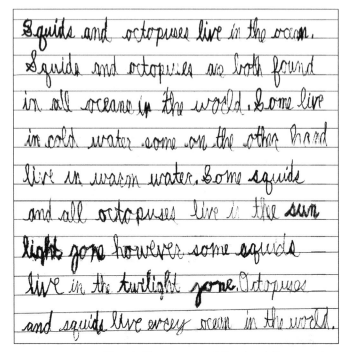

Evan's Compare and Contrast Paragraph

Evan:	Yes, I've decided to add the word *both* to this sentence. It says, "Squids and octopuses are found in all oceans in the world." I am going to change it like this, "Squids and octopuses are both found in all oceans in the world." I saw the word *both* on the chart and thought I could use it here.
Mrs. Gilpin:	That's a good word to use in that sentence. Could you share another change you're making?
Evan:	My next sentence says, "Some live in cold water and some live in warm water." I'm going to use *on the other hand*.
Mrs. Gilpin:	How are you going to use that phrase?
Evan:	Well, my new sentence will read, "Some live in cold water. Some, on the other hand, live in warm water."
Mrs. Gilpin:	Evan, the changes you are making will really help your reader to understand that you are showing similarities and differences between squid and octopuses and where they can be found in the ocean.

If you look at his paragraph shown above you will see he also used the word *however* in a sentence. His work is a great example of how a quick mini-lesson and conference can help students strengthen their writing. Although he was one of my stronger writers and his original paragraph was acceptable, through this lesson he was able to take it a step further.

SHARING TIME

During sharing I have students get into groups of three to five to share their paragraphs. The groups discuss which structure each paragraph follows by looking at the key words or phrases they contain.

Teaching Students to Conduct Short Research Projects © 2015 by Ryan K. Gilpin, Scholastic Teaching Resources

Lesson 16: Text Structures: Cause and Effect, Problem and Solution (3 Days)

Two additional key informational text structures are cause and effect and problem and solution. These structures present more complex relationships than the ones covered in the previous lesson and are more challenging for students to grasp, so I spend extra time on them. I've had success with this lesson, which incorporates some whole-class research on a topic related to our theme. If I can't find a text related to the theme that lends itself to examining these text structures, I will use text on a high-interest topic or current event.

Over the course of several days before teaching this lesson, I read aloud *The One and Only Ivan* by Katherine Applegate. This book tells the story of a gorilla who was captured as an infant and ended up living in a shopping mall in the United States for almost 30 years. Over the years, people became outraged at his treatment and demanded a change. When we finish the book, we research online and in books to find out more about gorillas and discover the fact that they are endangered. I create charts to record our learning, and we use these as we turn our focus to cause-and-effect and problem-and-solution text structures.

I break this lesson into two parts. On the first day I introduce these two text structures and add new information to our anchor chart from the previous lesson (Lesson 15). Then I have the students work in small groups on an activity where they examine problems for gorillas and the solutions to these problems, based on the information we learned from *The One and Only Ivan* and our class research. The next day, my students use the information they gathered during the activity to write a paragraph using either the cause-and-effect or problem-and-solution text structure. After completing these activities, students are ready to examine questions about their own animals to write new paragraphs using these two text structures.

MATERIALS

- Text Structure anchor chart from previous lesson and markers
- Research notes from whole-class research project (see above)
- Posterboard
- Text structure posters (see website on page 88)
- Paragraph graphic organizer (page 125)
- Conferencing notebook

Mini-Lesson: Day One

Mrs. Gilpin: Yesterday we began working on revising our paragraphs and looking at various text structures that authors use. We created a chart to use as a resource when writing, and today we will add two more text structures to that chart. On our chart we have *description, compare and contrast*, and *sequential*. Let's take a moment to review these and the key words you can use with these text structures.

We review the chart, and then I introduce the next two text structures.

Mrs. Gilpin:	There are two other structures authors use when writing nonfiction. These are *cause and effect* and *problem and solution*. When authors use cause and effect, they are often explaining an event that occurred and the reasons why it occurred. They are explaining why certain things happened. For example instead of writing, "The koala's habitat is getting smaller." I might write, "Many trees are being cut down to make roads, and because of this, koalas are losing their habitat." Some of the key words or phrases you might use are: *because, since, leads to, led to, therefore, as a result of, consequently, for this reason,* and *due to.*

As I list these words and phrases, I add them to our chart along with my example.

Mrs. Gilpin:	The last text structure we will look at is problem and solution. Authors use this structure to explain a problem and possible solutions to those problems. Some of the key words and phrases are the same as cause and effect because the two are very closely related. Some words and phrases often used when writing about problems and the solutions to those problems are *a solution, possible, the problem shows, consequently, because of,* and *as a result of.* For example, I might write about the koala's habitat being destroyed, "One problem koalas are currently facing is habitat destruction. This is because new roads are being built through the eucalyptus forests. A possible solution would be to protect these forests to prevent new roads from being built."

After completing the anchor chart with my students, I explain the activity they will be doing. To get them started, we review the research we completed on gorillas after reading the book The One and Only Ivan.

Mrs. Gilpin:	Today you are going to work on a group activity using information we gathered about gorillas. Before we get started, let's review some of that information. After we finished reading *Ivan*, we looked up information on the Internet and read a few books from the library about gorillas. What were some of the things we discovered about gorillas?
Aubrey:	They are endangered!
Beth:	Yeah, almost extinct!
Noah:	There aren't that many gorillas left in the world.
Greg:	Gorillas are in Africa.
Evelyn:	They are killed.
Evan:	Hunters and poachers are killing and hurting them.
Noah:	There have been wars that have hurt them.
Katy:	Farms are being built, and they are losing their homes.
Emily:	Yeah, the farmers are cutting down the trees.
Liam:	Weren't there fires or something?
Mrs. Gilpin:	Wow! You all remember a lot about what we learned! There are many

problems facing gorillas, and as a result they have become endangered. When we researched, we also read about some ideas to help keep gorillas from becoming extinct. There were two major problems facing gorillas that we learned about: habitat destruction and poaching and hunting. Today you're going to work in small groups, and each group will be assigned one of these problems. You will be given two pieces of posterboard. On one sheet you will write and illustrate the problem, and on the other sheet you will write and illustrate the solutions to that problem.

I divide the class into small groups and hand out the posterboard. As they begin working, I move through the room to discuss the problems and solutions with each group.

WORK TIME/CONFERENCING

Before I begin conferencing with groups, I give them time to get started and gather their ideas. Typically they are buzzing with energy so I don't like to interrupt their work until they have had a chance to really discuss what they are doing as group.

Mrs. Gilpin:	I've been listening to your discussion, and I'm curious to know more about what you all are doing.
Liam:	Well, we're looking at habitat destruction, and we know that there have been many farms built, and that they're taking the land from gorillas.
Evan:	And there have been wars, which have caused fires, we think. Those fires destroyed their homes too.
Katy:	They have cut down trees to make the farms. The gorillas live in the forests, so when they take the trees down the gorillas have no home.

I explain to the group again that they are to create a poster about this problem—and leave them to get started on it. I continue to go around the room and discuss with groups the problems and solutions. As groups are finishing up, I explain what they will be doing next.

Mrs. Gilpin:	I can see that everyone is almost done with their posters. In five minutes we will gather in our whole group area and each group will share the problems and solutions they discussed.

 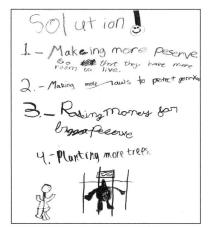

Problem-and-solution posters created by students

SHARING TIME

Once we gather as a class, each group presents their posters.

Noah:	Our group made posters about poaching and hunting gorillas.
Aubrey:	One of the problems is hunters. They will set traps and gorillas get caught in them. The hunters sometimes aren't hunting for gorillas, but they still get caught.
Evelyn:	The hunters sometimes hunt gorillas, but it's for their hands and feet and stuff. Like a trophy or something.
Noah:	They are called poachers. Poachers only take certain parts of the gorillas and sell them for money.
Emily:	A solution to this is new laws, like not letting the hunters there. It's not allowed.
Evelyn:	Yeah, like having no-hunting areas.
Noah:	There need to be more preserves for gorillas. A place that is safe for them where there is no hunting or poachers and there are people to help with that.
Mrs. Gilpin:	You all did a great job presenting the problems gorillas are facing, and you also shared some good solutions for how these problems are being solved or could be solved. Another way to think about these issues is cause and effect. For example, we know that the habitat of gorillas is shrinking. What caused that?
Pam:	People are cutting down trees where they live.
Robb:	They're making farms to grow food, so the gorillas can't live there anymore.
Mrs. Gilpin:	Yes. So one cause of the gorilla's habitat shrinking is that humans are cutting down trees for farming. Tomorrow we will use these posters, along with our anchor chart on text structures, to do some writing about gorillas and these problems.

Mini-Lesson: Day Two

Mrs. Gilpin:	For our projects, we have been working on our paragraphs by looking at text structures and the key words or phrases we can use to make our writing stronger. Yesterday we looked at problems for gorillas in Africa, we talked about what caused these problems and what some solutions for these problems might be, and you worked in small groups to create posters. Today we'll be using those as we do some more paragraph writing.

As a class, we review and discuss the posters they created the day before. Then we review the anchor chart, and I give students copies of the paragraph graphic organizer.

Mrs. Gilpin:	Now let's take a look at the text structure anchor chart. Yesterday we looked at cause and effect and problem and solution. When authors use cause and effect they're often explaining an event that occurred and the reasons why it occurred; they are explaining why certain things happened. When authors use the problem-and-solution text structure they are explaining a problem and possible solutions to that problem. Today you will work independently on a paragraph about an issue gorillas face, either with their habitat or about hunting and poaching. As you write, I want you to think about the key words and phrases you could use to strengthen your writing and what structure would make your meaning most clear. I'll give you a paragraph graphic organizer, and you can refer to the parts of a paragraph anchor chart on the wall. The posters you created are now hanging on the wall as well, and the text structure anchor chart is here on the easel. You have a lot of resources available to you as you work on this paragraph!

WORK TIME/CONFERENCING

As students get started I go around the room observing and taking notes.

Mrs. Gilpin:	Hi, Beth. Tell me about the writing you've done today.
Beth:	I'm almost done with my paragraph. I just need the closing sentence.
Mrs. Gilpin:	Explain to me what you've written about.
Beth:	I wrote about gorillas and the problems they have. I did the poaching. I did problem and solution and looked at the chart and used the words *because* and *as a result*.
Mrs. Gilpin:	Tell me how you went about getting started today.
Beth:	I did the organizer [*she gets the organizer and shows me*]. I decided the topic was about the gorilla being endangered. Then I did the details and the closing. Then I wrote the paragraph. I need to finish my closing sentence.
Mrs. Gilpin:	You go ahead and continue writing; I'll be back soon to read your finished paragraph.

I continue to check in with students about their writing. The overwhelming result of this activity is some of the best writing I have seen from my students.

Gorillas

Gorillas are endangered.
Endangered means almost extinct.
Gorillas are endangered for two
reasons. Poachers, and habitat
loss. As a result gorillas could
go extinct! Because of this, our
children mightn't know what a
gorilla is! We should help the
gorillas by stopping poaching,
writing letters to the
Government, and make more
preserves. Gorillas are
endangered, and they need our
help or Poachers will kill them
all.

Beth's problem-and-solution paragraph

Gorillas are endangered for many reasons. One reason is habitat destruction. However humans can help by having fundraisers so that governments can help gorillas by making preserves for them. Another reason is hunting and pouching. Humans illegally hunt gorillas and consequently gorillas numbers drop. If this keeps up gorillas will soon be extinct! Humans can help by making new laws about pouching. Gorillas are threatened and helped by humans.

A student's cause-and-effect paragraph about the whole-class research topic

SHARING TIME

During sharing time I have my students partner up or get into small groups. They share their paragraphs and peer edit their work so they can publish their pieces. Since this lesson's writing is often of such a high quality, I usually ask my students to type it up. Then I paste each of their paragraphs on a sheet of construction paper, laminate it, and put together a display for others to enjoy. After completing this lesson, it is a lot easier for my students to write about the animal each researched and what role humans are playing in the survival of the animal.

Mini-Lesson: Day 3

Mrs. Gilpin: Over the last couple of days, we've worked with problem-and-solution and cause-and-effect text structures. I was impressed with the paragraphs you wrote! Today we're going to turn back to our animal research projects, and I'd like you to think about whether you could use those text structures in any of your paragraphs as you revise.

For the rest of the workshop time, I confer with students as they revise their writing. At the end, I invite students to share what worked well for them during the day's writing.

Teaching Students to Conduct Short Research Projects © 2015 by Ryan K. Gilpin, Scholastic Teaching Resources

> Peregrine falcons almost got extinct once. Peregrine falcons ate birds that ate wheat that had chemicals such as DDT on them. This lead to peregrine falcons having fragile eggs that cracked before they were ready two hatch. Because of this, laws were passed and as a result peregrine falcons are a very populated bird.

A student's cause-and-effect paragraph about his selected animal for the research project

Assessment for Step Four: Put the Plan Into Action; Create the Product

During this part of the project, my focus for assessment is on student writing. I look at students' use of the writing process, paragraph writing, and their understanding of text structures.

The first thing I assess is whether my students are following the writing process independently or whether they need reminders from me. I also assess how well they were able to revise and edit their work after the mini-lessons. For example, one mini-lesson I typically teach focuses on commas in a series. I will then look to see if my students applied this skill, and my notes on what kind of assistance they needed to be successful.

When assessing paragraph writing, I look at their organizers to see whether, and how well, students used them. I then look to see if they have clear topic sentences, supporting details, and closing sentences.

When conferencing with students about text structure and looking over their writing, I look for how well each student was able to identify which text structure would work best for the information he or she was presenting and how well each student was able to use key words and phrases to support that text structure.

For all of these components, I also assess how well students used their notes to guide their writing.

Publishing and Sharing

The final step in any research project is sharing the results with others. Over the years, my students have done this in a variety of ways, depending on the project, but I always require the following basic elements: a display, published writing based on the student's completed research, and an oral presentation. This chapter presents lessons on publishing and presenting that strengthen students' listening and speaking skills.

Once students have revised and edited their drafts, they can begin to publish their actual product. Then they begin working on a display and presentation. Typically, my students are all at approximately the same stage in the writing process at this point. Sometimes, however, there are a few who have lagged behind the rest. As a result, I allow a two-week window for this phase of the project.

MAKING IT YOUR OWN

Publishing and sharing can take many forms, depending on the end product being created by your students. For example, students might choose to create videos or slideshow presentations to share their learning. Simply adapt the lessons to accommodate the particular forms your students are working with.

Chapter 5 Lessons

- Reviewing the Writing Process: Publish (1 Day)
- Public Speaking Skills (1 Day)
- Putting It All Together (1–2 Days)
- Sharing the Learning With Others (1 Day)
- Project Follow-Up and Reflection (1 Day)

Lesson 17: Reviewing the Writing Process: Publish (1 Day)

The last stage of the writing process is publishing. In this lesson I review with my students what publishing is and the steps they will take to complete their project.

I conference with every student early on in this part of the process to help them all get started and clarify any misunderstandings or questions they have. Since students have already planned what their final product will look like and have completed a draft, they have very few challenges as they reach this stage of the project.

MATERIALS

- Chart paper and markers
- Writing process anchor charts
- Research Project Publishing Checklist (page 126)
- Prepared materials for making a model publication
- Various types of paper and other materials for students to use for publishing
- Computers
- Conferencing notebook

Mini-Lesson

Mrs. Gilpin: Now that you have finished your drafts and have revised and edited them, you are ready to publish your work! I'd like to take a minute and review with you what publishing is. Let's take a look at our anchor chart and see what steps we take when publishing our work.

Mary: We finally get to make our books!

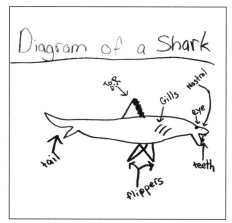
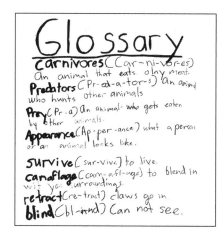

Sections of students' final copies

A CHEETAHS HABITAT

Cheetahs live in Africa. You can find some cheetahs in the savanna. Cheetahs rome through out the savanna. Some cheetahs live in Aisa. Cheetahs like to be in hot places. Cheetahs are mostly in eastern and sothern Africa.

Shelia:	We get to type and write the drafts over.
Eliza:	When we publish, we make sure to include the changes we made when we edited.
Mrs. Gilpin:	Yes, when publishing you are rewriting your work or typing up your work, making sure to include the changes and corrections you made when you revised and edited. For this project, everyone will be required to do some typing. Don't worry—you'll have some time in the computer lab as a class to do this, and we'll take turns using the classroom tablets.
Simon:	Do we get to illustrate now? I love drawing the pictures.
Doug:	Me too!
Mrs. Gilpin:	Part of publishing is illustrating. You will have the opportunity to draw the pictures you have in your plan. Some of you already sketched your illustrations. Now you will be able to color or paint them.
Dan:	Don't we make the cover too?
Mrs. Gilpin:	Part of your plan was to design your cover. While publishing, you will use your plan to create it.
Lisa:	I sketched mine when I drafted.
Mrs. Gilpin:	Many of you did a draft of your cover, which is going to help you when you begin publishing. In fact, your draft and your plan are going to be key to publishing successfully. Today I will go over the requirements of publishing, and I'll model for you how I'm getting started with my book on koalas.

I begin to model for my students how I use my plan and draft to begin creating my book.

Mrs. Gilpin:	Now that I have completed my research and written a draft of my book, I'm ready to publish. The first thing I need to do is to decide what type of paper I want to use for my book. Do I want to use regular computer paper, construction paper, tag board or posterboard cut in half, or notebook paper? I remember when I was working on my plan I wanted to make a big book, so I am going to cut tag board in half for my book.

I have a few pieces of tag board already cut so I can continue modeling.

Mrs. Gilpin:	I know I need to make my cover but I am going to do that last. I am going to look at my plan to see which page I have first. I see that I have my table of contents. I am going to go through my draft and find the table of contents. I am now ready to write the final copy of this page on my tag board.

I copy the writing from my draft onto the tag board as students watch. I will complete part of one more page to help students get an idea of how their plans and drafts work together to help them create their final copy. Then I'll review their requirements.

Mrs. Gilpin:	I am looking at my plan and I see after my table of contents I have my habitat section. For this section I have one page so I need one piece of tag board. I have a heading, a paragraph, a map, a fun fact. I am going to look at my draft again to find this page. On the plan I have

Teaching Students to Conduct Short Research Projects © 2015 by Ryan K. Gilpin, Scholastic Teaching Resources

the heading at the top of the page, and it's pretty big; so I will write my heading on the top of my tag board. I am going to use pencil so I can erase if I make a mistake; later I will go back over it with a marker. The next thing I notice on my plan is where the map is going. I see that I planned to make it about one quarter of the page. In my draft I only sketched a map of Australia, and I planned to shade in the eastern side of the continent.

I model drawing my map in pencil and note that I will go back and color it later. I tell students that I'm doing it this way because I'm modeling and if I colored everything it would take a long time. I explain that they can color their illustrations and other features as they are publishing.

I model writing one feature at a time, setting each one up the way I have it in my plan and copying the writing from my edited draft.

Student working on his final copy

Mrs. Gilpin: Today you will begin creating your final copy just like I did. To help with this, I have created a checklist to help guide you through this process.

I review the checklist before explaining what students will do during their writing time.

Mrs. Gilpin: I have added a lot of different types of paper to the writing center and have the larger tag board and posterboard on the reading table for you to choose from as you get started today. I will be coming around to check in with you to see how things are going as you begin to finish your projects.

WORK TIME/CONFERENCING

While students begin creating their final copies, I make sure to conference with each one to help set goals and clarify any questions. Typically my students work independently through this process with few challenges. Often students will realize they want to make a change to the final copy that wasn't in their plan, struggle with how to utilize their plan while making the final copy, or require help figuring out how many pieces of paper they need for their final copy. Some students feel overwhelmed and afraid they won't have enough time to finish. For this reason, I help students set goals and break them down into manageable steps. Some students will want to make changes to their writing at the last minute, and they'll ask to conference about those changes.

The following is a conference with a student who often struggled to keep up with the rest of the group. To assist him, I made sure to conference with him and set goals to help him complete the various parts of the publishing process.

Mrs. Gilpin: Hi, Adam. I see that you're starting to work on publishing your book. How is it going?

Adam: It's going well. I'm worried that I have to finish in two weeks though.

Mrs. Gilpin:	When you're working on a project it can feel a bit overwhelming when you have a deadline. When I feel this way, I set small goals for myself and work on a little bit at a time. Do you think setting some goals might help you in completing your project?
Adam:	I think so.
Mrs. Gilpin:	Great, Let's look at what you have left to do. It looks like you have completed your cover, table of contents, and the first page of your book. I see you have two pages for each section of your book and there are five sections. What would you think about completing one section each day?
Adam:	Well, that's about two pages a day. I think I can do that!
Mrs. Gilpin:	Great! I'm going to leave you to continue working, and I'll check back first thing tomorrow to see where you are. We can discuss your goal again then and decide if you still think it's going to work best for you.

Student using his plan and draft to begin his final copy

SHARING TIME

At the end of work time, I invite to students to share how things went with their publishing.

Mrs. Gilpin:	Today you began writing the final copies of your publications. How did it go?
Katy:	I was working on my table of contents, and it was pretty easy to do because I had my draft. I was basically copying my draft. I just had to make sure I wrote big enough to fill the space on the posterboard I'm using.
Beth:	Yeah, I had to erase a heading because I made it too small. It's kind of hard to make the pages because the plan is small and my book is big.
Evelyn:	It was easy! I made two pages today of my moose book.
Mrs. Gilpin:	What made that easy for you today, Evelyn?
Evelyn:	Well, I already did the writing. I just have to make the book.
Mrs. Gilpin:	I'd like for someone to share a challenge you had today.
Bill:	I had trouble with the book I'm making. I realized I need to add more illustrations to one page. Are we allowed to make changes?
Mrs. Gilpin:	Why do you need to add more illustrations to the page?
Bill:	When I finished the page it had a lot of blank space, and I want to add a picture.
Emily:	One of my pages is like that. Can I add a picture too?
Mrs. Gilpin:	I think that would be fine, just make sure you plan the picture

first. Really think about what picture would make sense on that page with the information you've included. Maybe you could draft a caption for it before adding it to your page, too. As you continue, you might get some new ideas or realize you want to add information to your project. That's fine, but I'd like you to take the time to draft or sketch it first. That way it will be just as strong as the writing you've already done. Even when I write and think I'm done with something, I'm always thinking of ways to make it better. I just make sure to draft it first and then add it to my writing.

Eliza: I'm excited to see mine when it's done!

Shelia: Me too! And we get to share them with other classes!

Mrs. Gilpin: I'm excited for you too! Over the next week or so, you'll be working on your final copies and then you'll begin to work on your presentations for the other classes. It's a very exciting time as we near the end of this project!

Lesson 18: Public Speaking Skills (1 Day)

As students are nearing the completion of their final copies, they begin to think about the next step—sharing their learning with others. To help prepare them for this, we discuss what makes a presentation interesting and how to give a good one. This lesson is brief, but I refer to it during conferences as students are preparing for their talk.

Public speaking helps students learn to articulate their ideas clearly and think about their audience—not just the information. It also builds confidence. The school where I teach requires all students, starting in kindergarten, to participate in a number of activities that involve speaking to an audience. Because of this, many of my students have a good idea of what they need to do in order to give a good presentation, and this knowledge is reflected in their responses in the discussion below.

MAKING IT YOUR OWN

Even if your students are not very familiar with public speaking, this is still a great lesson to conduct. Make sure to focus on getting kids familiar with the basic public speaking skills: being prepared and knowing the topic, making eye contact, and speaking clearly and loudly.

MATERIALS

- Chart paper and marker
- Conferencing notebook

Mini-Lesson

Mrs. Gilpin: As you are finishing up your final copies, I want to start thinking about the next step for this project, which is sharing your learning with others. We'll have other classes coming to visit soon, and you'll be presenting the information you researched to them. Today I want you to think about and discuss what good speakers or presenters do. Take a moment and think to yourself what you have noticed when someone presented something to you. What did they do well? What made it interesting?

As students take a moment to think, I write at the top of a piece of chart paper, "How to Give a Good Presentation."

Mrs. Gilpin:	As you share your thinking I'll create a list on this chart of things that help give a good presentation.
Aubrey:	When the eighth graders give their speeches, they talk loudly so we can all hear in the auditorium.
Page:	Yeah, I can always hear them. Well, sometimes they speak quietly, and then I don't hear them.
Mrs. Gilpin:	When giving a speech or speaking to an audience, it is important that everyone in the room hear you. This way all of the information you want to share and want people to learn about is heard. I am going to write on the chart, "Speak loud enough so everyone in the room can hear you." When speaking to an audience, you don't want to use a yelling voice, but you don't want to use your classroom voice either! You want to make sure your voice is strong and everyone hears you. You also want to make sure you speak clearly.
Katy:	Do you mean like not so fast? I remember one time there was a speech and the person talked so fast I didn't understand.
Mrs. Gilpin:	When speaking to an audience, you don't want to speak so fast that your audience doesn't understand you, but you also don't want to speak so slowly that your audience gets bored! Let's add this to our list.

On the chart I add, "Speak clearly—not too fast, not too slowly."

Noah:	Shouldn't you look at the audience?
Emily:	I sometimes look down. Seeing everyone look at me makes me nervous.
Mrs. Gilpin:	It is important to look at your audience when speaking. It helps keep them engaged in what you are sharing. Also, when you look down your voice will go in that direction. You want your voice to go to the audience, so looking up also helps with that. Let's add this idea to our chart.

On the chart I write, "Look at your audience. Make eye contact."

Mrs. Gilpin:	Something I do when preparing to speak to an audience is plan my talk. I like to take time and think about what I am going to say and the order I am going to present ideas in. I usually write key points in order on a notecard so I have something to look at if I forget what I want to say. But often just writing out the plan and knowing it's there is enough—I remember what I want to say! You will be given

Teaching Students to Conduct Short Research Projects © 2015 by Ryan K. Gilpin, Scholastic Teaching Resources

time to plan your presentation and what you want to say because it is important to be prepared. You all know your topics very well, but if you don't plan your presentation it may seem to your audience that you don't know a lot. Let's add this to our list as well.

On the chart I add, "Plan ahead. Know what you are going to say. Prepare your speech."

My next point is to introduce the idea of a display when presenting. When students finish their publications, I give them the opportunity to create something else to add to their display.

Mrs. Gilpin:	Another thing to start thinking about is what kind of visual display you will have. Everyone has written a nonfiction piece that will be part of the presentation, but what else would you like to create as a visual display about your topic? We'll talk more about this in the next lesson, but you can start thinking about it now.
Pam:	Like an illustration or painting?
Bill:	Or a diorama?
Mrs. Gilpin:	Yes, those are good ideas. You can add to your display once you have completed your final copy. What you choose to add is up to you. It just has to go along with your topic, and you need to incorporate it into your presentation. Having visuals for your audience or providing things they can interact with, like your nonfiction text or a diorama, will make your presentation more interesting and engaging.

On the chart I write, "Have a visual display."

My final point is one I feel is important to emphasize with students. They've worked incredibly hard and should feel proud of the work they have completed.

Mrs. Gilpin:	The final point I want to discuss with you is to be confident when you speak. You have worked very hard and put a lot of effort into this project. You know your topics well and have learned an enormous amount of information about your animals. You should feel good about this work and confident sharing what you know with others.
Maria:	I am really proud of my work and know a lot more about dolphins now!
Emily:	I have never worked this hard on something, I'm proud too.
Phil:	This was my best book ever.

These are often the comments I hear from my students when we're nearing the end of this project. Their sense of pride is astounding. They often feel that this project is the best thing they have ever done in school. To end the lesson, we review the list we created.

How to Give a Good Presentation

- Speak clearly – not too fast, not too slowly.

- Look at your audience. Make eye contact.

- Plan ahead. Know what you are going to say. Prepare your speech.

- Have a visual display.

- Be confident!

Anchor chart for public speaking

Mrs. Gilpin:	Let's take a look at our list and review what we have decided will help us give a good presentation. We need to speak loudly and clearly, look at the audience when speaking, plan ahead so we are prepared, have a visual display to help keep our audience engaged, and—most important—be confident!

Lesson 19: Putting It All Together (1–2 Days)

Once students have finished their final copies and we have discussed what makes a good presentation, they are ready to work on their presentations. At the end of this lesson, students will practice their presentation and share their final project with peers. I have found that each time a student presents his or her project, the student becomes more comfortable speaking in front of others and more confident making the presentation. This lesson can be done over one or two days. When I extend it over two days, I first create the chart that lists what to include in the presentation; then on the second day, I teach how to prepare a notecard for the presentation.

MAKING IT YOUR OWN

Depending on the project you have chosen to complete with your students, your list of requirements for a presentation may look different.

MATERIALS

- Posterboard
- Computers
- Various materials for students to use to create display pieces
- Index cards
- Conferencing notebook

Mini-Lesson

Mrs. Gilpin:	Now that you have finished your publications and we have discussed what helps make a good presentation, it's time to think about your presentation and what you will do when presenting your information to others. Today we'll discuss the requirements for your presentations, and then you will be given time to begin working on them!

My list of requirements is short and it gives students lots of choice in deciding how they'll go about putting their presentations together.

Mrs. Gilpin:	When we have the other classes visit, you will each give a short presentation to the whole group. Then those students will have the opportunity to visit your table and ask you questions, read your

Teaching Students to Conduct Short Research Projects © 2015 by Ryan K. Gilpin, Scholastic Teaching Resources

	pieces, and look at your display. Together, let's brainstorm some things you may want to include when presenting to the whole group. Take a moment and think about presentations you have seen.
Shelia:	I remember that the eighth graders set up a table with stuff about their speeches. Like the girl who did hers on horseback riding. She had her boots and helmet on the table and then she told us about them.
Mrs. Gilpin:	It sounds like you are remembering that some of the older students who gave speeches had props relating to their topic that they showed and explained to us.
Timmy:	I like when they have a table with stuff on it better than when they don't. It's fun to see stuff.
Mrs. Gilpin:	That's right, Timmy. As I mentioned yesterday, your presentation will be even more interesting if it includes some sort of visual display. So in addition to your written piece, I'd like you to create one other visual for your table. What are some ideas for a visual display?
Bill:	I want to do a diorama! I can have sand and little camels made from paper.
Noah:	Yeah, I want to do one for the falcon, like a city line.
Beth:	I want to do a big poster with a bunch of fun facts about cheetahs!
Katy:	I have a stuffed animal dolphin at home; can I bring that in? I think I can do a poster too, just a big diagram even though I have one in my book!
Mrs. Gilpin:	All of these are great ideas, and remember—having a display is one of your requirements.

On the chart I write, "Create one display piece."

Mrs. Gilpin:	The next thing I want you to think about is what you will say to your audience when it is your turn to present. What sort of things do you think you should include when presenting?
Emily:	I think what animal we researched.
Mrs. Gilpin:	Yes, you want to make sure you introduce your topic. We studied a lot about animals, but what was our focus?
Simon:	We looked at all of the things our animals need to survive.
Liza:	And how humans are helping animals. Also threats.
Mrs. Gilpin:	When you present, you will only have a few minutes each; that won't be enough time to present all of the things you learned, which is why we will have time for people to visit your table. When you present, you are going to want to keep it simple and only share a small portion of what you learned. I think introducing your animal and then giving three or four facts about what your animal needs to survive would be great! You could also share a little about the role humans play with your animal. I am going to write those ideas down.

On the chart I write, "Introduce your animal and the focus (survival)." I add, "Discuss the role humans play in the survival of your animal."

I require these two things because both are the key questions students were focusing on when researching. When the audience members visit students' tables, my students will be able to share more details and answer questions.

Pam:	Can we share one fun fact? I have this really cool fact about sharks that I think is interesting and want to share.
Evan:	Yes, I have one about squids.
Greg:	And I have one about snakes.
Mrs. Gilpin:	I think that is a great idea! There are some really interesting facts that we want to share that will help entertain the audience. I think it's a great idea to share one or two really cool facts that you think people will be interested in! I'm going to add that to our chart.

One the chart I write, "One or two fun or interesting facts about your animal."

Mrs. Gilpin:	Today you will begin working on your presentations and displays. Let's take a moment to review what you should each include in your presentation before you begin working. Today when planning, make sure you include introducing your animal, what your animal needs to survive, and what role humans play in your animal's survival. You also want to include some fun or interesting facts, and a visual of some kind to include with your publication.

Before sending my students off to work on their presentations, I go over one more thing, planning a notecard to have on hand while presenting. While explaining to students, I share with them my own notecard about koalas.

Mrs. Gilpin:	When presenting, you want to be prepared and have a plan for what you will share, but you don't want it to seem as though you are reading from a card or paper. One way to help with giving a presentation is to think about what key points you will share and write those down on a notecard in case you get nervous. You don't want to write everything you will say, but just a few words to help you remember.

I show students a notecard that I have put together for my presentation.

Mrs. Gilpin:	On my notecard about koalas, I write the words *Australia, eucalyptus forests,* and *marsupials* for when I introduce my animal. For the role humans play I wrote the phrases *roads being built* and *forests being cut down*. For my interesting facts I wrote *sleep up to 18 hours a day* and *use a grooming claw for bathing*. Although this isn't the exact speech I plan to give, these few notes will help me remember what I wanted to share with the audience. Today as you are working, I'd like you to put together a notecard that you will have when you present. I will be coming around to conference with you today, and together we can work on your notecard.

Teaching Students to Conduct Short Research Projects © 2015 by Ryan K. Gilpin, Scholastic Teaching Resources

WORK TIME/CONFERENCING

I conference with my students about what they're planning for their presentation and how to set up a notecard to use in case they get nervous or forget what they wanted to share.

Mrs. Gilpin: Hi, Mary. I see you're working on your notecard. Have you thought about what information you will share with the audience when it's your turn to speak?

Mary: I was thinking I would tell them a little about how pandas need to eat and they love bamboo, and they are in China in the conifer forests. The Chinese really love the panda and they have laws to help protect the bamboo forests.

Mrs. Gilpin: Have you thought about the fun facts or interesting facts you want to share?

Mary: I was thinking it should be something people might not know. Most people don't know that pandas are carnivores. They eat bamboo, they have adapted to eat bamboo, but they will eat small mammals too. I also want to share about the baby pandas that were born at the zoo since I got to see them on the camera the zoo had.

Mrs. Gilpin: Have you worked on your notecard yet?

Mary: Yes! I wrote *bamboo*, *China*, *conifer forests*, and *carnivores*. I also wrote *National Zoo baby pandas*.

Mrs. Gilpin: It sounds like your presentation is coming along nicely. Have you thought about the display piece you want to have with your publication?

Mary: I was wondering if I could use a computer tablet. I was wondering about an idea.

Mrs. Gilpin: What is your idea?

Mary: Since I used the panda cam at the zoo to watch the pandas, could I use one of the tablets to play it at my table while I present? I think it could be cool to show the other kids.

Mrs. Gilpin: That would be a great thing to add to your display! It would be really interesting for your audience to see real footage of the pandas at the zoo!

My next conference is with a student who is very nervous about presenting in front of an audience and isn't sure how to use the notecard.

Katy: Mrs. Gilpin, I'm really nervous about speaking in front of everyone.

Mrs. Gilpin: It's quite normal to feel nervous. I still get nervous when I'm presenting to other teachers in meetings! When I'm a bit nervous, I make a notecard that I can glance at while speaking, and I make sure to practice a few times beforehand so I'm comfortable and confident about what I'm going to share. Let's think about the information you want to present.

Katy: I wanted to share a little bit about dolphins, like where they live and what they eat.

Mrs. Gilpin:	Can you tell me a little bit about those two things?
Katy:	I want to share with everyone that dolphins live in the ocean but sometimes in freshwater too. They eat lots of little fish. I want to tell how much a day, and stuff like that.
Mrs. Gilpin:	Let's look at your notecard and write down some key words. It sounds like you want to start by sharing that dolphins are found in oceans and freshwater areas.
Katy:	I guess I should write down *oceans* and *freshwater*.

She writes these two things onto her notecard.

Mrs. Gilpin:	You also mentioned sharing what they eat and how much.
Katy:	Can I write that down on my card?
Mrs. Gilpin:	Yes. Now let's think about the fun or interesting facts you wanted to share.
Katy:	I think I am going to share about dolphin families being called a *pod*. Another funny thing I read was that there was once a dolphin who liked to yank feathers off of pelicans!
Mrs. Gilpin:	I think those are two very interesting facts to share, and I think you are doing quite well on your notecard. I want you to write down a few things about threats or the role humans play in the survival of dolphins that you want to share, and I'll check back with you in a few minutes.

When I check back with Katy, she has a completed notecard and we rehearse a little of what she is going to share. I have found that the notecard helps all students, but especially those who get nervous in front of an audience. Practicing one-on-one with students who are nervous also helps them become more comfortable with giving a presentation and build confidence.

SHARING TIME

Mrs. Gilpin:	Today for sharing time I would like you to partner up with someone and practice your presentation. Tomorrow we will practice presenting to the whole class, but for today I want you to practice with a partner.

Students pair up and begin practicing their presentations and giving feedback to one another. This is very similar to peer editing. Students should share one or two things they liked about the presentation and if there was anything they did not understand. I make sure to emphasize the importance of positive feedback and constructive criticism. Here are two students sharing their ideas.

Evan:	Did you know that squids and octopuses are invertebrates and live in all oceans around the world? They can live in different parts of the ocean like the twilight zone. The giant squid is huge! It can get up to 60 feet long! One thing that hurts squids and octopuses is trash. When people throw their trash in the water, it can kill the fish and other sea

Teaching Students to Conduct Short Research Projects © 2015 by Ryan K. Gilpin, Scholastic Teaching Resources

life. We can help by making sure not to litter when we are at the beach.

Liam: I like your fun fact! Can a squid really get that big?

Evan: Yes! That was the largest ever found. Most giant squids they have found are about 25 feet long.

Liam: I like your presentation. I think the other kids will think it's interesting, especially when they look at your brochure. I did the platypus. The platypus lives in and around Australia. They live in rivers and lakes. The platypus has two thick layers of fur for the colder weather. They live in burrows along the river, and their habitat is getting hurt. People are lining the rivers with cement, and then they can't live there.

Mrs. Gilpin: Great job today, class! Tomorrow we'll set up tables and you'll practice your presentations one or two times with each other. You will be able to ask each other questions and read one another's publications! Then on Friday we will have the fourth- and fifth-grade classes come to see your presentations!

Lesson 20: Sharing the Learning With Others (1 Day)

It's important for students to share their learning with others. Not only does it give a purpose to the research, it also helps them develop their public speaking skills and practice answering unforeseen questions. It requires them to take their new knowledge and use it meaningfully in conversations, and it gives them a sense of accomplishment and pride as they bring this project to a close.

Students sharing their projects with one another

MATERIALS

- Displays
- Publications
- Notecards

Mini-Lesson

Students setting up displays

Mrs. Gilpin: Today is presentation day! I am so excited for you to present your projects to an audience. You have worked so hard and know so much about your animals! You should be incredibly proud of what you have accomplished. Today you will be given some time to finish setting up your tables and practice your presentations before the other classes arrive. Make sure you have your notecard, publication, and display piece ready to go.

I give students about 25–30 minutes to set up their displays, visit their classmates' displays, and practice their presentations before the other classes arrive. Once the other classes are settled, I introduce the project, and my students begin presenting. Each student conducts a short presentation to the whole group, and then the other classes are given the opportunity to visit each student to look at the projects and ask questions. Below are three examples of the short presentations.

Beth: Cheetahs are amazing animals. They live in Africa and Asia. Cheetahs are carnivores, which means they only eat meat. They stalk their prey and then chase and pounce to catch it. Did you know a cheetah can run 60–70 miles per hour? Cheetahs are close to becoming endangered because of poachers. People hunt the cheetah for their fur. There should be more laws making it hard for poachers to kill cheetahs.

Beau: My animal is the warthog. The warthog lives in the savanna in Africa. It is hot there in the summer. They look fierce but they aren't. They do not like to fight. Did you know the warthog's name in Swahili is *ngiri*? We should protect the warthog's habitat so they do not become extinct. If they became extinct future kids might not get to see them.

Greg: Snakes are cool. Snakes can have many colors. Some are black and gray and others are red and yellow. Snakes are aggressive eaters and chase their prey then swallow it whole! Did you know snakes eat up to 30 meals a year? Some people are afraid of snakes and kill them. They are sometimes more afraid of you. To help snakes to survive we shouldn't kill them.

In the following exchanges, my students field questions from Tanisha, a fourth grader, and Nora and Max, two fifth graders.

Tanisha: Hi, Emily! I like your book about squirrels! I didn't know they can't be found in Australia.

Emily: Yeah, they can be found in North America, South America, Asia, and Africa but not in Australia or Antarctica!

Tanisha: What kind of homes do they have?

Emily: They have nests, dens, and burrows. Sometimes they will take over an old bird's nest. They use grass, leaves, and feathers to build their homes.

Nora: Lea, I love your poster about beavers. I did a book about dolphins when I was in third grade! Can you tell me more about beavers?

Lea: The beaver is a rodent! It's related to squirrels, mice, and rats!

Nora: Wow! I didn't know that! Where do beavers live?

Lea: They live in a lot of places. They live in North America, Asia, and Europe. They live here too. I saw a dam on the river when I was with my dad. They chop down trees along the river to make their dams.

The next student had written a magazine about bees.

Tim: Extra! Extra! Read all about it! Did you know that a bee hive is made from beeswax? The cells in a hive are used for storing honey and laying eggs!

Max: Where are honey bees found?

Tim: They are on every continent except Antarctica. It's too cold for flowers there.

Max: I heard the honey bees are dying!

Tim: Yes! They aren't really sure why, but they think it's a disease. If bees die, the plants can't survive. The bees help pollinate the flowers.

Older students with younger students

Project Follow-Up and Reflection

The final step in any research project is reflecting on the process. I encourage students to think back over their work and consider all that they've learned, not only about their topic, but about how to generate questions, search for answers, record information, write about their learning, and share their work with others.

Mrs. Gilpin:	Yesterday, you all did a fantastic job presenting your projects to others. I received numerous e-mails from teachers and other adults sharing how impressed they were with your work and how much you knew about your animals. Today we are going to take some time to reflect on what you learned about doing research and writing during this project. I'd like for you to take a moment and think of one thing you learned during this project. Then turn to your neighbor and share.

I give students a few minutes to talk with a partner.

Mrs. Gilpin:	I'd love for you to share with the class what you learned about writing. I'll make a list on chart paper.
Simon:	Text structure. Like sequential and compare and contrast.
Evan:	Yes. I used compare and contrast. I never used that before.
Nick:	I learned about paragraph writing.
Aubrey:	Oh yeah, with topic sentences and details, and a closing sentence!
Emily:	I learned about researching. I learned how to find information and how to figure out if it was good.
Beth:	I learned it helps to plan my writing. Doing the plan helped when I did my draft and final copy.

Typically the list my students generate is pretty extensive and shows they have learned a lot about doing research and writing nonfiction. Once the list is complete I give them their assignment.

Mrs. Gilpin:	Today during your work time I would like you to write a letter to me reflecting on your learning. I want you to take time and really think about everything you learned during this project about nonfiction writing and doing research. You don't need to write about your animal and what you learned—you did that already! Just focus on what you know about writing and doing research.

Once students have completed their writing they can share with the class what they wrote.

Assessment for Step Five: Present and Share the Learning

For this last part of the project I assess two things: students' final copies of their writing and the quality of their presentations. In their final copies, I look at how well they used their plan and drafts as guides. I also look at the overall level of creativity in their projects. During their presentations I assess their public speaking skills and how well they were able to answer audience questions.

Teaching Students to Conduct Short Research Projects © 2015 by Ryan K. Gilpin, Scholastic Teaching Resources

Appendix

Designing Your Own Research Projects

Over the years I've done the animal project numerous times with great success, which has led me to incorporate more research projects into my curriculum. No matter what the topic, I follow the same process to design and teach these units; the steps are summarized below:

1. Narrow the focus and develop a key question.
2. Conduct the research.
3. Create a plan for the product.
4. Put the plan into action; create the product.
5. Present and share the learning.

Two of my favorite research projects have been a study of the *Titanic* and a unit on biographies. What follows is a brief explanation of how I completed these projects, following the same five steps above. Incorporating student choice is key, and the possibilities for writing about and presenting research are numerous—please do not be limited by my suggestions! On page 127, you'll find a planning template you can use to develop your own units.

Titanic Museum

For this project, my students create a museum all about the *Titanic*. My goal is for each student to individually create a display for the museum that contains pieces of writing explaining the display. Students also work with a partner or group to create a separate display and writing piece for the museum.

1. NARROW THE FOCUS AND DEVELOP A KEY QUESTION(S).

Students first start by reading all about the *Titanic*. I conduct reading groups using various nonfiction and fiction books and provide materials for independent reading. Students then narrow their focus by choosing one aspect of the *Titanic* they're interested in learning more about; for example, students might choose to research the crew, the three passenger classes, the various rooms, food and entertainment, how the ship sank, the discovery of the wreckage, the people who were on board, and so on.

Students choose one topic to research independently, and another topic to research with a group. I developed the following key questions for this project:

- Should the *Titanic* wreckage site be protected?
- Why are people so fascinated with such a tragic event?

2. CONDUCT THE RESEARCH.

Students begin researching their chosen topics, taking notes and gathering information. They use both print and digital resources—and evaluate and document those resources. As a whole group, we conduct research about the wreckage site and events surrounding its discovery in order to form an opinion about one of the key questions: Should the *Titanic* wreckage be protected?

3. CREATE A PLAN FOR THE PRODUCT.

Students put together a plan for their museum display. This might include a plan for artifacts, models, visuals, digital media, and graphic organizers for the writing. They also create a list of supplies needed for the creation of their products. They may sketch what they want their display to look like.

4. PUT THE PLAN INTO ACTION; CREATE THE PRODUCT.

The fourth step for this project is to create the museum displays and draft, revise, edit, and publish the writing that will go with each display. This step typically requires the most time, as students might be building a replica or reproducing some other artifacts that could be found in a *Titanic* museum. Then, as a class, we put the museum together, and students practice their presentations.

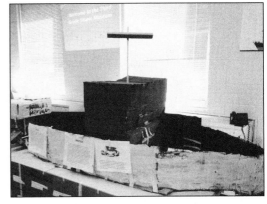

Student display for Titanic *museum— Bob Ballard's Ship*

5. PRESENT AND SHARE THE LEARNING

The final step is for students to share their learning with others. We open the museum at different times, inviting other classes, administration, and parents to visit. The students present to the audience in groups, sharing the displays they created together. After all of the groups present, the audience members can go around the museum and ask students questions about the displays they created individually.

Biography Interview Project

For this research project, my students each select a person they're interested in learning more about. After gathering lots of information about this person, each creates a display that includes an illustrated timeline of his or her subject's life and writes a biography of the subject. Each student also dresses up as this person and participates in an interview, answering questions from the audience as the person he or she researched.

1. NARROW THE FOCUS AND DEVELOP A KEY QUESTION.

Students start by reading many different biographies. They do this in both their independent reading and in reading groups. They each then select a person they're interested in learning more about, and we begin discussing as a class the subtopics they will be researching: childhood, family life, education, challenges, accomplishments, important dates. We also develop the key questions:

- Why is this person important?

- How did this person influence the world?

2. CONDUCT THE RESEARCH.

In the next step, students begin researching their chosen person. They take notes and gather information from both print and digital resources and evaluate and document those sources.

3. CREATE A PLAN FOR THE PRODUCT.

For this project, students are required to create a display about the person each researched—an illustrated timeline of that person's life, and a biography that answers the key questions: Why is this person important? How did this person influence the world? During this part of the process, each creates a plan for what to include in the display, an outline or layout of what the illustrated timeline will look like, and an outline for the biography.

At this stage they also plan their costumes, in preparation for their interviews. During the interviews, they'll dress as their research subjects and answer questions from the audience.

4. PUT THE PLAN INTO ACTION; CREATE THE PRODUCT.

At this point, students draft, revise, edit, and publish the required writing piece for the project. They then follow the writing process for the illustrated timeline. Students also put together their displays and costumes. Students are given time to create notecards to help with the interview part of their presentations.

Student dressed as Amelia Earhart for Interview project

5. PRESENT AND SHARE THE LEARNING.

In the final step of this project, students present what they've learned to an audience. They are given an opportunity to share a little about the person they studied, and then they participate in an interview, taking on the persona of their subject and answering questions from the audience. The audience has been handed questions in advance, so the students are familiar with the questions they might be asked. After the interviews, the audience is given time to visit each student's display and ask further questions.

Project Possibilities

As you can see, there are numerous options for planning and presenting research. Here I will summarize a few formats that I have used; I hope this list sparks some ideas, and I encourage you to add to it!

PLANNING TOOLS

* graphic organizers
* outlines
* storyboards
* notecards

DISPLAY OPTIONS

* collage
* diagram
* diorama
* illustration
* map
* museum display
* prop
* slideshow

WRITTEN OPTIONS

* advertisement
* blog
* book
* brochure
* diary
* editorial
* feature article
* flapbook
* magazine
* museum display description
* newscast
* newspaper
* podcast (with script)
* poster
* powerpoint presentation
* scrapbook
* video (with script)

Name: _____

Assessment Checklist

SKILLS & OBJECTIVES	NOTES
Choosing a topic	
Evaluating sources	
Note-taking	
Documenting sources	
Choosing a type of writing	
Creating a plan	
Using the writing process	
Paragraph writing	
Using text structure, key words, and phrases	
Final copy	
Presentation	

Name: _____

Note-Taking Form

Topic: _____ Subtopic: _____

NOTES OR FACTS I FOUND	TITLE OF THE BOOK OR WEBSITE	PAGE WHERE I FOUND THE INFORMATION

Name: _____

Bibliography

Books

TITLE	AUTHOR

Magazines

TITLE AND AUTHOR	MAGAZINE AND ISSUE DATE

Websites

WEBSITE NAME	URL

Name: _____

Writing-Process Checklist

Draft

☐   I used my notes and plan to guide my draft.

☐   I have drafted each nonfiction feature from my plan.

☐   I have drafted each paragraph.

Revise

☐   I have read my draft through at least two times.

☐   I have organized my writing in a meaningful way.

☐   I have worked on my paragraphs to make sure I have a clear topic sentence, details, and a closing sentence.

☐   I had a friend read my work and I asked for feedback.

Edit

☐   I have checked spelling.

☐   I have checked punctuation.

☐   I have checked for capital letters.

☐   I had a friend edit my work when I was done.

Name: _____

Paragraph Graphic Organizer

Topic:

> [ ]

Topic Sentence (Focus or Main Idea):

> [ ]

The Body (3–5 Details):

> [ ]

> [ ]

> [ ]

> [ ]

> [ ]

Closing Sentence:

> [ ]

Name: _____

Publishing Checklist

☐   I used my plan to help write each page or section of my final copy.

☐   I used my draft to help write each page or section of my final copy.

☐   I made sure to include the changes I made to my writing while revising and editing.

☐   I typed at least one page or section of my final copy.

☐   I read my final copy at least two times before turning it in.

☐   If there was more writing I wanted to add, I drafted it first.

Name: _____

Research Project Planning Sheet

Research Topic: _____

Key Question(s): _____

_____

_____

What will students create? _____

_____

_____

How will students create their end products? What materials and resources will they need? _____

_____

_____

How will students share their learning with others? _____

_____

_____

How will I assess student learning? _____

_____

_____

Resources

Applegate, K. (2012). *The one and only Ivan.* New York: HarperCollins.

Beck, I. L., McKeown, M. G., & Kucan, L. (2002). *Bringing words to life: Robust vocabulary instruction.* New York: Guilford.

Calkins, L. M. (2003). *Launching the writing workshop.* Portsmouth, NH: Heinemann.

Calkins, L., Ehrenworth, M., & Lehman, C. (2013). *Pathways to the Common Core: Accelerating Achievement.* Portsmouth, NH: Heinemann.

Collier, L. (2013). Nell Duke on reading and writing informational texts—keys to student success. *Council Chronicle, 23,* 18–21.

Common Core State Standards Initiative. Retrieved from www.corestandards.org.

Duke, N. K. & Bennett-Armistead, V. S. (2003). *Reading & writing informational text in the primary grades: Research-based practices.* New York: Scholastic.

Fisher, D. & Frey, N. (2013). A range of writing across the content areas. *The Reading Teacher, 67,* 96–101.

Fountas, I. C. & Pinnell, G. S. (2001). *Guiding readers and writers: Teaching comprehension, genre, and content literacy.* Portsmouth, NH: Heinemann.

Harvey, S. & Goudvis, A. (2007). *Strategies that work: Teaching comprehension for understanding and engagement.* Portland, ME: Stenhouse.

Hoyt, L. (2011). *Crafting nonfiction: Lessons on writing process, traits, and craft.* Portsmouth, NH; Firsthand.

Kalman, B. (2002). *The life cycle of a koala.* New York: Crabtree.

Larmer, J. (2009). *PBL Starter Kit: To-the-Point Advice, Tools, and Tips for Your First Project in Middle or High School.* Novato, CA. Buck Institute for Education.

Leograndis, D. (2008). *Launching the writers workshop: A step-by-step guide in photographs.* New York. Scholastic.

Maloch, B. & Horsey, M. (2013). Living inquiry: Learning from and about informational texts in a second-grade classroom. *The Reading Teacher, 66,* 475–485.

Newingham, B. (2011, March 24). My March Top Ten List: Nonfiction Reading Resources. Retrieved from http://www.scholastic.com/teachers/top_teaching/2011/03/my-march-top-ten-list-nonfiction-reading-resources.

Owocki, G. (2012). *The Common Core lesson book, K–5: Working with increasingly complex literature, informational text, and foundational reading skills.* Portsmouth, NH: Heinemann.

Pinnell, G. S. & Fountas, I. C. (2007). *The continuum of literacy learning: A guide to teaching.* Portsmouth, NH: Heinemann.

Robb, L. (2004). *Teaching nonfiction writing: A practical guide: Strategies and tips from leading authors translated into classroom-tested lessons.* New York: Scholastic.

Shanahan, T. (2013). You want me to read what?! *Educational Leadership, 71,* 10–15.

Stephens, K. E. (2008). A quick guide to selecting great informational books for young children. *The Reading Teacher, 61,* 488–490.

Zhang, S., Duke, N.K., & Jiménez, L.M. (2011). The WWWDOT approach to improving students' critical evaluation of websites. *The Reading Teacher, 65*(2), 160–168.